architectural details

architectural details

a home source book of interior fixtures,
from taps to tiles, doors to floors

MAGGIE STEVENSON *with photography by* CHRIS EVERARD

RYLAND
PETERS
& SMALL

LONDON NEW YORK

Senior designer **Sally Powell**

Senior editor **Sophie Bevan**

Location research **Kate Brunt and Georgia Stratton**

Picture researcher **Emily Westlake**

Production **Tamsin Curwood**

Art director **Gabriella Le Grazie**

Publishing director **Alison Starling**

First published in the United Kingdom in 2002 by
Ryland Peters & Small
Kirkman House
12–14 Whitfield Street
London W1T 2RP
www.rylandpeters.com

10 9 8 7 6 5 4 3 2

ISBN 1 84172 323 1

A CIP record for this book is available from the British Library.

The publishers cannot accept liability for any injury, damage or loss to
person or property, direct or inconsequential, arising from suggestions
made in this book. The publishers recommend that any structural,
electrical, or plumbing work is carried out by a qualified professional.

Printed and bound in China.

CONTENTS

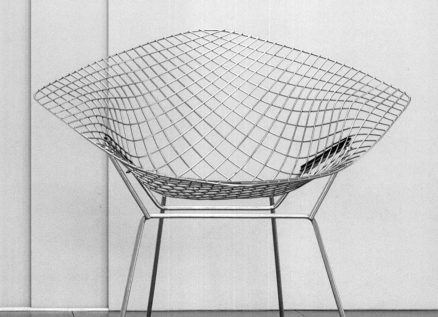

introduction

Architectural details define and underline the style of a home. They can be seen in the fabric of the building – the walls, ceilings, windows and staircases – where they create a context for the decorating scheme. And they are there in the finishing touches – the door handles, light fittings, taps and tiles – without which no scheme would gel. Most of these things are interesting or beautiful in their own right, many fulfil a specific function, but it is always the way they are used and their appropriateness to the scheme that is important.

Architects and designers know where to find the materials and fittings they need to create or restore interesting interiors and, in this book, they reveal their sources. Eclectic in their shopping habits, they will buy as readily from high-street stores and builders' merchants as from specialist suppliers, so if the item you want is not listed in the directory at the back of this book, you could easily find it in a local shop. Some of the names in the directory are trade suppliers who do not sell direct to the public but will deal with the builder or tradesperson you employ. Usually items are only made available to the trade because specialist knowledge is needed for their installation. Obviously, complex lighting systems and structural features such as staircases require specialist specification and installation, but even something as apparently straightforward as a marble worktop for a kitchen is best left to an experienced fitter as inaccurate measuring could prove to be an expensive mistake.

Because individual shops will be inaccessible to the majority of readers, most of the items are listed in the directory under the name of their manufacturer. Most manufacturers (but not

all) deal only with retailers, but should be able to direct you to a mail-order supplier or a local shop where you can buy their products. If the manufacturer is based overseas, call or check their website for details of agents or suppliers in your home country. Makers who do not have international distribution may be willing to ship their products overseas but (with electrical and plumbing fittings in particular) make sure you will be able to install them safely and legally when they arrive.

Some products become recognized as design classics because they combine form and function successfully and strike a chord with contemporary taste. Favoured by architects and specifiers, you'll see them crop up in different settings throughout this book. Often, these classics are not as contemporary as they look and were conceived by Modernist architects and designers in the mid-20th century. One advantage of their enduring popularity is that they are likely to remain in production for the foreseeable future, while designs with a less distinguished pedigree will be superseded or simply disappear.

Designers restoring period buildings often frequent architectural salvage yards in their search for authentic fixtures and fittings. Although they are a reliable source, the quality of merchandise is variable and it pays to establish whether the item you are buying is complete and in working order, as spare parts and an experienced repairer may be hard to find later on. If absolute authenticity is not a priority, some of the larger salvage specialists sell reproduction pieces – specifically radiators, bathroom fittings and brassware – copied from originals that have passed through their hands.

This book is intended to be as much a source of inspiration as information. The images offer hundreds of ideas for imaginative interiors, while the directory will help you realise them.

DOORS & WINDOWS

DOORS AND WINDOWS ARE INTEGRAL TO A HOUSE. PART OF ITS ORIGINAL CONCEPTION, THEY ARE DESIGNED IN PROPORTION TO ITS SIZE AND FASHIONED TO COMPLEMENT ITS CHARACTER. IN MOST CASES THERE IS LITTLE TO BE GAINED FROM ALTERING THESE FEATURES, AND SOMETIMES MUCH TO BE LOST. HOWEVER, IN HOMES THAT ARE BEING EXTENDED OR CONVERTED, OR ARE UNDERGOING A RADICAL REDESIGN OF THE INTERNAL SPACE, NEW DOORS AND WINDOWS CAN UNDOUBTEDLY IMPROVE THE LIVING SPACE.

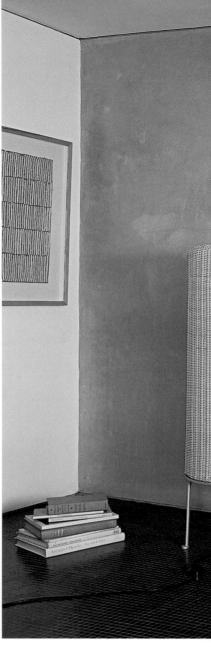

doorways

The front door is the main feature in the façade of a house and is designed in proportion to the building – consider the narrow doors of tall Georgian terraces, the wide doors of Victorian villas and the broad flat canopies and flush doors of 20th-century Modernist houses. Factors determining the proportions of interior doors are slightly different, being as much to do with the importance and purpose of the rooms they connect as with the style of the building.

above left **Double doors make an imposing entrance, but these understated doors are at one with the quietly contemporary hallway.**
above centre **A huge single door, its thickness in proportion to its size, pivots slightly off-centre, converting an existing archway into a doorway.**
above right **Due to its exaggerated height, this double doorway has the proportions of a standard contemporary single door.**

The door is the first feature of any house, apartment or room with which you make direct contact. You focus on it as you approach, see it at close quarters, and then touch it as you enter. How it looks, feels and works are key to the way it integrates with its surroundings and to the first impression you have of the space you are entering.

Size is the first thing you notice about a door and this may be decided for practical or aesthetic reasons – ideally both factors will be taken into consideration. In a seaside cottage, for example, the doors may be small to conserve heat. By contrast, in a converted industrial building they will be much larger than usual to allow for the passage of goods, machinery and the increased traffic of a workplace. In townhouses, the conventional format for doors – developed from the 18th-century rules of proportion

– required the height of a door to be a little more than twice its width. Now there are no such limitations and though the standard size is more likely to be two-and-a-half times taller than it is wide, doors can be made to order in any shape or size.

Conventionally, the doors of the most important and public rooms – usually those leading off the entrance hall – were the largest, heaviest and most decorative, possibly including a wide architrave, moulded panelling and sometimes pilasters and pediments. The doors on upper floors, less often seen by guests, were much simpler. Such conventions may seem anachronistic in a modern home, but although times have changed the status factor still holds good, and living-room doors tend to be more impressive in size, style or quality than in other rooms.

door styles & materials

At one time doors were made from oak and little else, but later softwoods such as fir, spruce and deal became the norm and were frequently painted to imitate costlier timbers. Now, the materials used to make doors are much more varied, with softwoods, hardwoods, plywoods, metal and glass all competing for popularity.

opposite, above left **Separating a loft apartment from the central staircase, this Japanese-inspired sliding door has an ash frame glazed with a single pane of glass and suspended from a beam.**
opposite, above right **The vertical lights in this door are in Arts and Crafts style. The glazing bars of the outward-opening exterior door are similarly geometric.**
opposite, below left **A flush sliding door glides across a wide doorway. The recessed pull is the only interruption to the smooth expanse of door and wall.**
opposite, below centre **Over-doors – decorative wood pediments – were a familiar feature in prosperous houses of the late 19th century. This one is rather**

taller than usual and forms part of a suite of carved panelling in a house of the Aesthetic Movement.
opposite, below right **This red oak door was custom designed by Mark Pynn with square panels to reflect a square motif used elsewhere in the house. The doorknob, made from oil-rubbed bronze, conforms to this theme with a specially made square escutcheon.**
this page, below left **In hot climates or high summer, the heat of direct sun through glazed doors is unwelcome. In this Singapore house a louvred panel, its vanes fixed in the horizontal position, holds the balance of light and heat, allowing most light to pass through when the sun is low in the sky.**

this page, below centre **An unusual surface for an interior wall, these horizontal planks with the bark left on give a modern rustic look. Continued across the door with perfect alignment, the camouflage is so effective that when the door is closed, the door handle is the only obvious clue to its presence.**
this page, below right **These country-style doors belong to a house that was once a working farm building. The old doors, in too poor a condition to salvage, were copied exactly, but the lintel above the door has survived intact and still bears the original limewash. The paint colour chosen for the doors is Powder Blue by Farrow & Ball.**

left **Old, but probably not original to the Georgian house in which it is found, this four-panelled door, painted a soft grey-blue, is typically Victorian in style.**

below left **Tongue-and-groove panelling is not usually associated with contemporary interiors but by painting the wall boards a dramatically dark colour and the door a pale cream tonally related to the wooden island unit, the scheme separates into modern blocks of contrasting colour.**

below centre **Painting the doors and walls on this landing the same sunny yellow gives a sense of space and continuity, with white architraves providing sparking highlights. Unusually, the doors are fitted with thumb latches instead of knobs – a detail that lends a rustic touch.**

below right **Derived from the abstract paintings of the American artist Ellsworth Kelly, the arrowhead shape of this tangerine MDF sliding door suggests movement.**

right **What strikes you first about the doors in this loft apartment is their colour. The cupboard doors are made from light blue MDF and the sliding door separating the living room from the corridor beyond is bright yellow. However, the most interesting thing is that the sliding door is certified as a fire door, as it is most unusual for sliding doors to gain this approval. When closed, a weight-and-pulley system pushes the solid-core timber door against seals hidden within the door frame, rendering it smokeproof.**

The most popular modern wooden doors are those in softwood or solid or veneered hardwood. They may have clear or semi-opaque glazed panels to allow light to spill from room to room. Others are made from plywood in a hollow box construction or from a composite wood material such as MDF, which provides a perfectly smooth base for a painted finish and can be cut into unconventional shapes. Metal frames have been a feature of external doors since the 1930s, and the pioneering manufacturer Crittall is still in existence today producing metal door and window frames in similar patterns to the originals, for those renovating Moderne houses or adopting that style.

Large metal-framed exterior doors containing a single pane of glass often form part of contemporary houses and extensions, allowing daylight to pour in and enhancing the feeling of space by visually merging the interior and exterior. Internal glass doors usually have a wood or metal frame and solid glazing bars to indicate their

this page, above **The entrance to this room within a room is more moveable wall than door and, when closed, there is no obvious point of access. The sandblasted glass panels are held in aluminium frames, two of which slide on small castors along tracks recessed into the floor.**

this page, below **These pivoting double-glazed 'barn doors' by Metal UK span one end of a living room. The narrow galvanized-steel frames emphasize the double square shape and are appropriately discreet in a room with no skirting boards or other applied decoration.**

opposite, above left **Sliding doors with dark mahogany frames and white glass panels have an oriental appearance reminiscent of Japanese shoji screens.**

opposite, above centre and right **Sliding doors in the glass walls of this garden pavilion draw back wide to unite the indoor and outdoor spaces. When the sun is at its height, Venetian blinds drop down over doors and walls. Flush fittings give a smooth finish: the sliding track fits level with the floor and the the lock is recessed into the aluminium frame.**

opposite, centre left **The Kyoto sliding partition by Eclectics is made from sheer fabric panels to bring a feeling of openness. More a screen than a door, it defines rather than encloses space.**

opposite, below left **Crittall steel doors usually have a distinctly retro look. Here, however, there is a shift in perception as the bare galvanized metal harmonizes with the cool neutral tones of the materials in this modern kitchen.**

opposite, below right **Dark, handsome wenge – the designer wood of choice – forms the frame for translucent glass sliding doors. The materials link the two areas: the pearly sandblasted glass with the oyster-coloured sofa; the dark timber frame matches the hall furniture.**

presence. However, in some contemporary interiors, frameless panels of toughened and usually frosted glass are suspended from a sliding track on the ceiling as a sleek and minimalist alternative to the conventional hinged door.

Most doors are still hung on hinges and open inwards, but this arrangement can be reversed to give more usable space inside the room, provided there is enough space outside for the door to open safely. Doors that divide rooms are traditionally hinged in pairs but, again, if space is limited, bi-fold doors or sliding doors may be a more practical option. Sliding doors come into their own as room dividers: when closed they offer privacy and bring the intimacy of individual rooms; opened up they create expanded, sociable spaces for larger gatherings. However, they have the disadvantage of requiring blank wall space, free of pictures and furniture, on which to open. One solution to this is to construct a false wall in front of the original one so the opening door slides between the two and is completely concealed when open.

top row, far left **Cabinet handles that pull to open must be shaped or textured so they do not slip through your fingers. The neat grey and nickel knobs on these cupboards are from the Forges range designed by Eero Aarnio for Valli and Valli and have a velvety matt finish to ensure a secure grip.**

top row, centre left **A sliding door requires a flush handle and, when it is a bathroom door, the handle must be lockable, too. A recessed bathroom indicator bolt like this one by Merit Metal has one fold-flat handle to open the door and turn the lock.**

top row, centre right **Projecting door handles can be annoying – and even hazardous – in a small bathroom where there is little space to undress or towel dry. A flush ring handle – sometimes known as a squash-court ring – is a safe and stylish solution, and is available from Saturn Hardware.**

top row, near left **Cabinets and drawers in a contemporary kitchen require minimal but functional fittings that are in keeping with other furnishings in the room. This softly curved matt nickel pull handle by Häfele fits the bill.**

handles & pulls

Hardware for doors and drawers is essentially functional, but alongside its main purpose it has an important stylistic role, too.

You'll know you've selected the right hardware for your home when you no longer notice it. Well-chosen fittings are visually in harmony with their surroundings, perfectly integrated with the door or furniture they open and smoothly efficient in operation. Make the wrong choice and every time you enter a room or open a cupboard you will be aware of the jarring mismatch of style, the way the handle sticks when you turn it or feels uncomfortable to hold. Instead of being automatic, the normal process of moving around your home and using the things in it will become an effort.

middle row, far left **Contrasting materials add interest to a simple design. Components in the Sembla collection by Allgood, from which this propeller handle comes, are available in grey-finished, polished or matt stainless steel and can be combined in any permutation.**

middle row, centre left **A wide, contoured handle is comfortable to hold and looks good against a plain door. A modern classic designed by Johannes Potente in 1953, the 1020 design in aluminium or brass is from the FSB range by Allgood.**

middle row, centre right **The slim, curved profile of this Ecostile satin chrome lever handle by Valli and Valli is in perfect visual balance with the glazed door.**

middle row, near left **Spherical doorknobs have a satisfying weight and substance and suit modern and traditional doors. The brushed chrome 1023 ball mortice knob from Nu-line comes in a choice of finishes.**

bottom row, far left **Unusual handles can be made from fittings designed for another purpose. In this kitchen, yacht cleats have been used on drawers and cupboards. Cleats are available from any chandler.**

bottom row, centre left **D-handles are universal. Available from all architectural ironmongers, they come in a variety of sizes and finishes – from polished metal to coloured nylon – and fit vertically or horizontally on doors and furniture alike.**

bottom row, centre right **This leather handle matches the door panel and lends a masculine character to the piece. Beautifully engineered runners ensure the leather is not put under too much stress.**

bottom row, near left **Quarter-round pulls are sturdy fittings for drawers storing heavy kitchen utensils. You'll find them in a variety of finishes at DIY stores and architectural ironmongers. Bright chrome or a softer nickel finish give a modern look.**

windows

As natural portals for daylight and fresh air, windows are essential to our feeling of well-being. Viewed from the inside, they are a link between private space and the world outside, framing aspects of our surroundings in cameos that change with the time of day and the seasons. From the outside, they are probably the most distinctive feature of the buildings we inhabit, and they regulate the urban landscape with their repeating patterns.

Windows are part of the design of a building and essential to its integrity. If they are not a direct indicator of its age, status and purpose, they are at least a clue. Most Georgian and Victorian houses were built with wooden sliding sash windows, but hinged casements returned to favour with the Arts and Crafts movement and were followed in the 1930s by steel casement windows. Plastic window frames appeared in the 1960s but have never been able to shake off their budget image.

In older buildings, original windowpanes are as important and worthy of preservation as the frames that hold them, demonstrating their history by their gauge, colour and subtle grain. Old glass may not have the perfect, blemish-free clarity of modern glass, but the slight flaws within it cast rippling reflections on interior walls that bestow character and an atmosphere of calm.

Before technology allowed glass to be made in panes large enough to glaze picture windows, bay windows were built to allow more light to enter. By the 1930s, this concept had been refined in the shape of Suntrap windows, whose curved panes and streamlined, linear shape dominated popular domestic architecture. Now, glass technology allows windows to be made in any reasonable size. In modern houses,

above left **Casement windows are a typical feature of old working buildings and though this studio is now a living space and office, the windows survive as evidence of its previous incarnations as a coach house and, it is said, a falconry. The frames are wooden, though metal ones are not unusual in such a situation, and the glass is reeded, which has a prismatic effect.**

above centre **In houses which retain their original windows, their style is a useful guide to the age of the building. Sash windows became widespread in Britain and the U.S. by the 1720s and remained fashionable for** around 200 years, but their shape and the arrangement of the panes varied throughout that time. The thin glazing bars and gothic detailing in these windows are typical of the early 19th century. Also typical are the internal shutters which can be stored in the recessed shutter boxes at the sides by day.

above right **Oculi, or small round or oval windows, were a popular feature of 17th-century houses and reappeared in 1930s Modernist houses as porthole windows. This one pivots to open, but others contain an opening square casement within the arrangement of glazing bars.**

where glass forms the skin of the building, it is hard to know where walls end and windows begin. For the person inside, there is no confusion: the walls are windows.

With double-glazing and central heating to take care of the practicalities of keeping warm, it is easy to understand the attractions of a house where most of the walls are glazed. The view, the light and the feeling of space are undeniably seductive, but on the downside are the feeling of exposure and the contradiction of being within a landscape but separated from it. In houses within a rural or seaside landscape, the problem of being on display is less pressing than in town, as large windows and glass walls are usually positioned to gaze onto an open aspect where development is unlikely or impossible. In town, where privacy is a much rarer commodity, careful orientation and screening with trees, hedges or high garden walls is the answer. The feeling of separation that comes from viewing an outdoor landscape from behind glass is easy to dispel by creating a middle ground between inside and outside in the shape of a balcony, deck or terrace. Doors from the living area opening directly onto this space allow the scents and sounds of the garden, sea or countryside to be enjoyed with the view.

opposite, above left **Metal-framed windows with pivoting casements** were once common in schools, hospitals, the service areas of some houses and industrial buildings, like this converted factory. The frames are now glazed with frosted panes which give a clean groomed look, block the view without resort to blinds, and diffuse light into the bright white interior.

opposite, above centre **One advantage of high-rise living is that windows can be left uncurtained to give spectacular views without compromising privacy.** At night, when the scene changes to an illuminated cityscape, this contemporary apartment is placed securely in its urban context. The squared grid of mullions and transoms echoes the angular style of the furniture and is therefore an important element of the room's design, but some may find bare windows uncomfortable and prefer to soften the effect with gauzy, translucent blinds.

opposite, centre **Although the strong horizontal bias of this wall of windows recalls the Modernist architecture of the 1930s,** it actually forms part of a house designed in the last decade by Moore Ruble Yudell. With the Pacific Ocean on one side and a highway on the other, the decision to build the beachside aspect almost entirely of glass was easy to reach. The windows slide back to give access to a wide wooden deck, creating a huge open living area, while the horizontal panes and the deck rail outside add a strong nautical flavour.

opposite, above right **A single, dramatic architectural feature can transform any building, however modest, into a local landmark.** This tiny house in a leafy Parisian courtyard was converted from a 19th-century storeroom by architect Damien Roland. Originally windowless, it has been made light by replacing sections of roof and wall with glass. Most striking of all these insertions is a huge circular window above the entrance which, at night, glows like a harvest moon through the trees.

opposite, below **The living area of this house, designed by Sidnam Petrone Gartner and set in the wooded landscape of upstate New York, is enclosed by glass,** making the already lofty space seem even greater. The boundary may be transparent but its steel structure is apparent, dividing the glass into panels of different sizes, each framing a detail of the surroundings.

above right **A series of tall, slender panels forms a shimmering crescent of glass that is part wall, part window.** A wall in as much as it forms a permanent and immovable division between house and garden; a window by virtue of the view it gives of the lawn and the countryside beyond. The curve of glass allows daylight to flood the indoor living space of this family home designed by Ken Shuttleworth.

centre right **The panoramic view at the junction of two glazed walls makes a strong connection between house and forest,** but switch your focus to the regular framework of the structure and the distinction between civilized space and wilderness becomes apparent. In summer, the glass is shaded by the trees, but in winter, sun filters through the bare branches to brighten the room through the daylight hours.

below right **Few homes enjoy such a broad, uninterrupted sea view, so this one exploits its position with a wall of glass.** The horizontal panes continue across the wall and door, emphasizing the strong parallel lines of the shore, wall and horizon.

above far left **Light entering this dining room is filtered first through foliage and then through the frosted windowpanes to give the space a bright but cool atmosphere. The window itself is left uncurtained, its regular geometry providing a framework for the shadow-show of plants brushing its outside surface.**

above centre **A wall of floor-to-ceiling windows can restrict the arrangement of furniture, but here the windows are raised from the floor, permitting low furniture to be placed below sill level. The long, narrow window accentuates the length of the room, an effect exaggerated by the dark fascia above.**

above **Daylight and privacy do not always go hand in hand, but in this bedroom a solution has been found by obscuring the central panels of glass in the window wall with frosted glass and constructing part of the flanking wall with glass bricks. Both materials screen the view effectively but otherwise have quite different effects: the frosted glass diffuses the light so it appears bright even on cloudy days; the bricks create rippling watery reflections when the light glints through them.**

left **The wall of glass separating the interior of this house from the terrace is virtually frameless. Rising from ground to ceiling with no visible means of attachment to either, the panels are joined side by side with the narrowest of vertical supports and are fixed and permanent. Outside, a slatted canopy overhangs the roof to shade the glass and, though it protects the interior from glare efficiently, the bars of shadow it casts on the terrace suggest pure heat.**

opposite, above left **Glass-to-glass assembly, the panes joined with narrow seams of mastic, means this fixed roof light offers a clear view of the sky.**

opposite, above centre **In an internal room, the shock of light from a large skylight is dramatic. The effect is heightened in this hall by leaving the room virtually bare of furniture, with a large oil painting as the only decoration.**

opposite, above right **A huge skylight ensures this studio apartment is always well lit. The sleeping platform suspended beneath acts as a baffle, protecting the space from direct sun. Operated by remote control, the skylight by Sunfold Systems opens for ventilation and to give access to the roof.**

opposite, below **VX Design and Architecture installed this large skylight to define the dining area in a free-flowing living space. A box containing storage and the extractor vent lowers the ceiling over a kitchen island and provides hanging space for a grass painting by Andy Harper.**

above right **This steel-framed glass roof is motorized to slide back and forth, transforming the dining room it covers into an indoor–outdoor space. Even when closed, its glazed sloping sides ensure good light all day as the sun moves across the sky.**

above far right **This extension is built in a familiar lean-to style, but that is where resemblance to any traditional construction ends. The exterior wall is a seamless pane, and the sloping glass roof supported by beams of laminated glass. At ground level, sections of the floor have been replaced with glazed strips to act as skylights for the basement.**

below right **A dining extension, built to mirror the adjoining kitchen, has matching steel-framed Crittall doors and a glass roof, designed and made by a conservatory company.**

skylights

By opening a room to the heavens, skylights admit maximum daylight and give the appearance of expanding the interior space.

The installation of a window in the roof is a sure way to fill the room below with natural light. Causing less visual disruption to the architecture than an additional window in the building's façade and much less likely to be overshadowed by trees or overlooked by neighbours, it admits light throughout the day. Skylights take many forms, from a simple polycarbonate dome admitting a shaft of light into a dark landing to a large panel replacing a section of the roof. Some skylights are fixed but, as extra sunlight inevitably results in increased heat, ventilation is essential for a comfortable environment. The familiar Velux windows commonly used in loft conversions open easily on a pivot, but other types are hinged or slide open. The inaccessibility of high windows means that a special opening system will be needed – this can be manually or electrically operated or automatically controlled by thermostat. Horizontal or sloping skylights must be fitted with laminated or toughened safety glass to protect against damage from high winds or falling masonry, and where overheating is a particular problem, tinted or solar-reflective glass will reduce the sun's glare.

blinds & shutters

Blinds or shutters are good choices for window coverings, controlling light and giving privacy without obscuring the architectural features.

First conceived to protect furnishings from fading in sunlight and as a security measure, shutters can be made to measure for modern windows with fixed or pivoting louvres or solid panels.

Blinds offer enormous scope across their range. Roller blinds are the cheapest and easiest option, and come in a variety of materials to give the perfect balance of light and privacy. Venetian blinds are even more flexible, with slats that can be adjusted to control the influx of light. Slats come in various widths, materials and finishes to suit virtually any size or style of window.

above **Metallic Venetian blinds are a good choice of window treatment for a kitchen, where steel and aluminium surfaces predominate. Narrow slats suit the proportions of a small window.**

near right **In a kitchen with one long wall of window, a purpose-made screen composed of etched-glass panels obscures the view and reduces glare. Each panel is separately mounted on steel brackets and pivots to alter the balance of light, but even when closed, the effect is cool and translucent.**

far right **Venetian blinds drop down over the glass walls and sliding doors of a garden pavilion to cool the interior on sunny days and give the walls solidity when the seclusion of an enclosed space is required. Separate blinds allow for the doorway to be left open while the windows remain covered.**

below near right **As well as dividing external and internal spaces, blinds can form a boundary within a room to give a degree of visual separation. Here a wooden Venetian blind is hung from a beam to screen the entrance from the sitting room without losing any sense of space.**

below far right **A city-centre apartment won't always have a pleasing outlook and, tilted just enough to allow sufficient light to enter, the half-opened slats of a Venetian blind are a smart visual distraction from the view.**

opposite **Pivoting curves of birch-veneered glass are an architect's solution to the problem of screening a huge window overlooking city rooftops while maintaining the level of light. At night the effect is not lost, as fine fluorescent tubes concealed within the panels take the place of daylight.**

FLOORING

AFTER THE WALLS AND CEILING, THE FLOOR IS THE LARGEST SURFACE IN A

ROOM. WHETHER COVERED OR LEFT BARE, ITS STYLE, COLOUR AND TEXTURE

WILL EXERT A STRONG INFLUENCE ON THE WIDER DECORATIVE SCHEME. OF

EQUAL IMPORTANCE IS THE WAY THE FLOOR FEELS. IT IS THE ONE SURFACE

WITH WHICH WE MAKE DIRECT CONTACT MOST OF THE TIME. WE WALK ON

IT, SIT ON IT, STEP OUT OF BED ONTO IT – SO, SOFT OR SMOOTH, IT MUST

BE COMFORTABLE AND PLEASANT TO TOUCH.

hard flooring

Claimed as the surface of choice for contemporary interiors, hard floors – from mellow flagstones to shiny metal, smooth terrazzo to chunky cobbles – have a long history.

Natural stone and ancient manmade materials like brick, mosaic, terracotta and ceramic have been used in ordinary homes for thousands of years and are still relevant today. Marble, slate and granite endowed the grand houses of the past with a sense of stability and sophistication and now bring those qualities to modern homes. Even concrete and metal, once deemed too utilitarian for domestic life, have been embraced by designers for their practicality and urban aesthetic. Add to these the glamorous terrazzo floors, frequently used in shops and hotels but equally appropriate at home, and the newly developed textural resin-based materials that mimic gravelly outdoor surfaces, and the list of hard floor options is longer than ever before.

All hard floors are rigid and comparatively heavy, so must be laid onto a level, stable sub-floor that is strong enough to bear the weight. A solid concrete base is the ideal, but wooden floors, properly reinforced and levelled, can provide a firm foundation. If there is any risk of movement in the sub-floor that could cause tiles or stones to crack,

above far left **More often seen in commercial interiors, terrazzo makes a very hardwearing floor, performing well in living rooms and other busy areas of the home. This example, in a warm honey colour, is semi-polished and fully sealed to give a low-maintenance satin finish. Fitted with underfloor heating, it is comfortable to walk on in winter and refreshingly cool in summer.**
above centre left **Smooth grey-green stone, like this Brazilian Camborne slate, has a matt surface that is durable, easy to maintain and perfect for through routes such as hallways and stairs. Had the steps been constructed entirely from grey slate, the effect would have been dark and heavy, but alternating slate treads with white-painted risers gives definition to the steps and a lighter, sharper look.**
above centre **Unpolished concrete is a sympathetic material for a modern country interior and a hardwearing non-slip choice for a hallway and staircase. Its grey-beige colour complements neutral schemes and provides a quiet background against which stronger colours can stand out.**
above centre right **Slate is a supremely versatile surfacing**

material and can be applied to vertical and horizontal surfaces in both wet and dry areas. In this contemporary bathroom, gleaming green slate tiles cover the floor, and larger panels line the shower enclosure to give continuity. Stone surfaces can be slippery when wet, so use mats inside and outside the shower.
above far right **More often seen as an outdoor surface, these beach pebbles set into cement make an unusual cobbled floor for a bathroom. As long as the stones chosen are smooth, rounded and do not stand too proud, they will be pleasantly stimulating to walk on with bare feet.**
near right, above and below **Chips of marble set in resin produce a continuous floor with a granular but level surface that is extremely durable. Laid in situ, the pale, slightly sparkling surface reflects light, making the room seem brighter and more spacious.**
far right **Metal flooring consolidates the retro-commercial design of this stylish home-work space furnished largely with vintage office furniture. In such a setting, the material's two main disadvantages – that it is slippery when wet and noisy underfoot – are not major concerns.**

above far left **Tough and elemental, a concrete floor is appropriate for an industrial-style kitchen, adding to its workmanlike style.** The smooth, compacted 'polished' finish is achieved by power-trowelling the wet concrete during installation. This is best done during the construction (ideally, before the walls are built) or during a major refurbishment of the building. When the floor is completely dry, a seal may be applied to protect against dirt and grease.

above centre **Pale Batigue Blue limestone tiles from Granite & Marble International present a cool background for modern metal furniture.** The tiles extend through to the kitchen where, for continuity, a worktop has been made from the same stone.

above near left **A favourite flooring for shops, office foyers, cafés and other public areas, smart, durable terrazzo is a good choice for the home, too.** Terrazzo tiles are easy to lay and give a uniform colour and pattern.

below far left **The mellow tones of brick paviors ensure their popularity in traditional homes,** but in a brighter shade of red, laid in an unconventional arrangement and edged with a contrasting material such as white marble, they take on a much more contemporary look.

below centre **Smooth terrazzo, laid in situ, is an elegant flooring for an open-plan space.** It is practical in the kitchen and looks sleek in the living area where rugs will soften its sometimes austere appearance. Installation is a professional job: the wet cement and aggregate mix is spread onto a stable sub-floor then ground and polished to a satiny finish. The resulting floor requires little maintenance beyond sweeping and occasional mopping.

below near left **Not just for utilitarian areas, pale concrete provides a sophisticated base for a modern neutral scheme.** The surface must be sealed to protect it from dust, but a matt finish gives it a softer appearance.

then expansion joints may be incorporated. Don't economize on installation, as the standard of preparation and finish has a bearing on the life expectancy of a hard floor as well as its appearance. Where the bedding material offers poor support or the joints are uneven, tiles and stones will eventually crack, chip or crumble.

The main problem associated with hard flooring is that it feels chilly underfoot, but this can be solved by underfloor heating. Installing this type of heating need not cause major disruption. Often an existing central-heating system can be adapted or extended to provide it or, if the room in question is a bathroom or other small room, an electric under-tile system can be put in independently from the main central heating. Once the floor is warm, the whole surface radiates a low level of heat, ensuring the room maintains a comfortable, even temperature.

If you're considering hard flooring, you will already have an idea of the effect you want to achieve, but factors other than style must be taken into account when you decide what flooring material to

top left **Old terracotta tiles are more often inherited than acquired, and a chequered floor has a time-worn charm worth preserving. Resist any temptation to protect old tiles with a waterproof seal, as moisture rising through the porous clay will cause the surface finish to deteriorate.**

top centre **A variation of terrazzo, this highly decorative flooring is made from Japanese river pebbles set into concrete then ground smooth. Its polished, randomly patterned surface contrasts with the plain, pale timber alongside it. Similar pebble flooring is made to order by Steve Charles.**

above left **A classic flooring pattern of light-coloured octagonal tiles linked by small dark keystones can be interpreted in stone or ceramic and in varying proportions to produce different effects.**

above centre **Colourful Victorian tessellated floors demonstrate the decorative possibilities of combining tiles of different shapes, but this floor gives the idea a modern slant by restricting the design to two colours and shapes and concentrating on the geometry of a 'tumbling blocks' patchwork. Similar terracotta tiles are available from Paris Ceramics.**

main picture and right **Frost-proof terracotta tiles can be used inside or out, and when continued through French doors onto a terrace they appear to extend the living space. Small patterned inset tiles add points of colour to the floor and allow a more interesting stepped layout. Large terracotta tiles are widely available and 50-mm-square glazed inset tiles from Turkey and Mexico are available from a range at Fired Earth. As the glazed tiles are less**

hardwearing than the clay, they should be slightly countersunk to reduce the wear they get.

opposite, above right **These new cement tiles have a darkly subtle colour and dead-matt finish that gives an impression of great age. The central motif, quartered at the corners, is a traditional device in tile design that results in a regular pattern when the tiles are laid. Made in Morocco, they are designed by Agnès Emery for Emery & Cie.**

opposite, below right **Grid designs of greater detail and definition can be produced with smaller tiles. These tiles, smaller than standard size but larger than mosaic, have a slightly metallic glaze which, together with the black border, gives a crisp, urban look. Similar 47-mm-square tiles are available from the Pro Architectura range by Villeroy & Boch.**

buy. Cost is always important and, with stone and tiles, the price per square metre is only part of the story. To get an accurate forecast, your calculations should include the cost of preparing the sub-floor, laying the floor and, if necessary, sealing it.

Practicality is another deciding factor. Be aware of the characteristics of different flooring materials and be realistic about how your intended floor will perform in the setting you have in mind. Granite and marble are hardwearing but marble can be marked by acids, and refinishing it is a professional job. Both are considered luxury materials and priced accordingly, so they are generally used in areas where their sophisticated good looks can be fully appreciated. Slate is another hardwearing stone, and is waterproof and stain resistant. More affordable than granite or marble and appropriate for both traditional and contemporary settings, it can be used to great effect in spaces such as kitchens,

39

hallways and staircases. All hard stones may be polished, but the higher the gloss, the more slippery the surface, especially when wet.

Softer stones like limestone and sandstone come in elegant neutral colours that are easy to live with. They are, however, porous and will stain if not sealed. Tiles vary in character and performance according to their type and quality. Bricks, terracotta and quarry tiles are all hardwearing, relatively inexpensive, easy to maintain and seem to improve in appearance with age and use. Traditionally used for kitchen flooring, they work well in other downstairs areas where a rustic look is required. Glazed tiles can look spectacularly colourful but not all are tough enough to provide a durable floor surface, so check before you buy. Less

opposite **An area of glass floor situated directly beneath a large roof light allows daylight to reach the basement of this potentially dark two-level building remodelled by architect Damien Roland. Although clear glass admits maximum light, it can be disconcerting to walk on so, to give a sense of solidity without losing light, the clear glass panels inserted into a central section of the floor were surrounded with more substantial -looking semi-opaque glass bricks. Viewed from below, the clear glass floor panels appear as a skylight, banishing the gloom so often associated with subterranean rooms. From above, the eye can rest on the surface, watching reflections, or gaze through it to glimpse the activity in the basement.**

above left **In a small mews house designed by architects McDowell & Benedetti, a glass walkway linking the upper rooms illuminates the enclosed staircase**

below with daylight and gives a lofty, spacious feel to the ground floor. To counter the slipperiness of the glass – and any feeling of stepping into the void – a series of friction bars has been sandblasted into its surface.

centre left **Designed as a showcase for shells and corals gathered in the West Indies, this floor is composed of white-painted boxes held within a steel frame, each covered with laminated glass. The boxes are lit by concealed fittings and the glass can be lifted, using glaziers' suction pads, to allow the contents to be rearranged.**

below left **There are situations where semi-opaque glass is more appropriate than clear. It gives privacy, defines boundaries and diffuses light, reducing glare. Irregular panels of ice-green frosted glass form the walls and floor of this passageway so it benefits from light entering from below and from adjoining rooms without affording a clear view in.**

robust tiles can be used in bathrooms where they will not suffer excessive wear, but wall tiles should never be laid on the floor.

Terrazzo and polished concrete floors are durable enough to perform well in most areas of the home, but installing them is specialized work and best done when a building is being constructed or during major refurbishment. Terrazzo tiles, which are thinner and lighter than in-situ terrazzo, can be laid with much less disruption and give a similar effect.

Metal floors have become more accessible with the advent of floor tiles, but if you are choosing sheet metal, it must be firmly fixed to a level sub-floor. Metal is very slippery when wet and should only be used in dry areas or for decorative effect in combination with another flooring material.

Glass floors look stunning, creating a feeling of space and allowing light to pass through different levels of a building. They are made from layers of annealed float glass (as opposed to sheet or plate glass) laminated together to provide the required strength. The surface is then sandblasted to render it slip resistant. Glass floors should always be professionally specified and fitted.

above left **A hard, closely grained timber, Canadian maple is often used for flooring in areas of heavy wear, so is perfect for busy areas of a home. Available from specialist suppliers, it can vary in colour from pale cream to brown – sometimes with a pinkish tone like the floor in this sunny room – depending on the part of the tree from which the wood was cut. The highest grade of maple is very light in colour with few, if any, small knots.**

above centre **The honey-coloured beech flooring installed in the living area of this open-plan loft apartment contrasts in colour and texture with the Treadmaster cork-and-rubber material in the kitchen beyond. Made by Junckers, the beech flooring overlays existing old pine floorboards. An expanded foam sheet between the two gives resilience and adds a degree of sound insulation.**

left **Plywood often displays a more exuberant grain than ordinary plank wood and can be cut into much wider boards which, in turn, show off its**

wooden flooring

Wooden flooring has never gone out of style. Its warm colour and flowing grain present a surface that is easy on the eye, warm underfoot and a versatile background for a variety of decorating styles. It occupies the middle ground between hard and soft flooring. More forgiving, resilient and quieter than stone or ceramic, and cooler and airier than carpet – wood offers the best of both worlds.

The wonderful thing about wood is its variety. It comes in natural tones ranging from white blond through every shade of brown to almost black, with a similarly wide diversity of grain patterns depending on the species of tree. Versatile in use, it can be laid in planks, strips or blocks in any number of geometric patterns, or used as the raw material for other wood products such as plywood and chipboard. It can reveal its own grain or be stained or painted to give colour.

Like most natural materials, wood improves with age, acquiring a deeper, more mellow tone, and old wood floors, scrubbed or waxed, complement traditional, rustic and contemporary interiors alike. In an old house, the easiest and cheapest way to acquire an old wood floor is simply to take up the carpets and expose the existing boards. Restoring old floorboards is not complicated but it is hard work and, if you don't wish to tackle it yourself, you can engage a specialist company to do the job. Provided the boards are free of rot or insect attack, are reasonably level and do not have wide gaps between them, the restoration process is simply a matter of securing loose boards, sanding down the surface and sealing it with one of the many proprietary solvent- or water-based products available. If it is necessary to replace damaged boards, reclaimed ones from an architectural salvage centre are likely to be a closer match in terms of colour, width and thickness than new. Old parquet floors can be restored in much the same way, but the blocks should be sanded in the direction of the grain to ensure a smooth finish.

wonderful pattern. A heavily figured ply like this Wisa spruce is most effective in a large room where its lively design, enriched and emphasized by a polyurethane lacquer finish, will not overwhelm the space.

above Reclaimed woodblock flooring gives a room instant character. Here it has been laid in a brick arrangement instead of the usual herringbone or basketweave pattern. Architectural salvage specialists usually stock blocks in a variety of timbers, including pine, oak, beech and mahogany, but often they need to be cleaned of old adhesive before being relaid.

right Wide boards give an expansive look, enhanced in this minimalist space by continuing the timber up to form a plinth for the cabinets that extend along the length of the room. The 200-mm-wide beech laminate boards were specially made, but can be ordered from Mafi. The raised platform at the end of the room is made from a light grey limestone which complements the warm colour of the wood.

left **The segmented floor in this curved hallway is composed of MDF panels painted chocolate brown. The edges of each panel have been chamfered to accentuate the radiating joints.**

opposite, above left **Chipboard is more often laid as a smooth base for another flooring, but these tiles – part of a floor-levelling system made by Kingspan Access Floors – have been lacquered and left uncovered. The tiles are supported on 'feet' which can be adjusted to compensate for irregularities in the floor surface. Galvanized metal fixings are visible at the corners of each tile and contrast nicely with the brown board.**

opposite, above centre **Old floors, whether original or salvaged, will lose some of their antique character if over-restored. Avoid aggressive sanding and be prepared to live with a slightly uneven surface and some gaps between boards. Maintain a natural look by scrubbing and waxing the boards or sealing with a clear matt varnish.**

opposite, above right **Sterling board, a coarse-grained form of chipboard, may not be as durable as some solid or laminated wood floors, but its warm golden colour and cork-like appearance are attractive and it is a fraction of the price of solid wood. Because of its weight, tiles are easier to handle than larger panels.**

opposite, main **Light oak boards in a room with a coastal view echo the colour of the sand. Although the tone is uniform, the boards are of differing widths to give a more interesting effect. Strong, durable, pest- and rot-resistant, and with a pleasing grain, oak is a classic flooring timber and looks wonderful in a contemporary setting.**

left and below left **A double border of darker wood inset in a parquet floor outlines the shape of this hallway and lends distinction to the pine woodblocks.**

bottom left **Reclaimed narrow woodblocks have been laid in rows and thoroughly sanded for a perfectly smooth, level and unusually striped floor.**

below right **End-grain woodblocks are supremely durable (they were used for the treads of 19th-century railway bridges and,** more recently, in the foyer at the Barbican in London). These are made from smoked oak – a rich dark wood.

bottom right **Parquet is usually glued in place but if it must be nailed down, the nails should be perfectly aligned.**

right **Practical, hardwearing and attractive, oak parquet extends throughout this basement kitchen and living area. The pale-toned wood was chosen to blend with the softly muted colour scheme.**

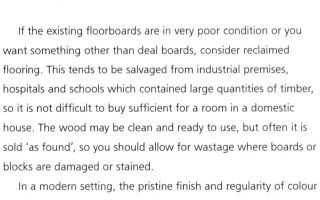

If the existing floorboards are in very poor condition or you want something other than deal boards, consider reclaimed flooring. This tends to be salvaged from industrial premises, hospitals and schools which contained large quantities of timber, so it is not difficult to buy sufficient for a room in a domestic house. The wood may be clean and ready to use, but often it is sold 'as found', so you should allow for wastage where boards or blocks are damaged or stained.

In a modern setting, the pristine finish and regularity of colour and grain that new wood provides may be more appropriate than a time-worn look. Popular and widely available timbers include pale hardwoods like maple, ash and beech which have a light, clean look, and cherry, walnut and oak which come in deeper wood tones. New wood flooring is sold in the form of solid boards, 'engineered' plankwood or as veneered boards.

...wood is the most expensive but it is also ... durable. It comes in various widths ... from narrow strips to boards of 200 mm or more. When solid wood shows signs of wear and tear, it can be sanded down and refinished.

Plankwood is composed of three layers. The top one, which varies in thickness depending on the maker, forms the surface of the finished floor; the central core consists of wood strips or blocks laid at right angles to this; and the lower layer runs in the same direction as the top. This type of floor is less expensive than solid wood, but it is extremely stable and can be made from timbers that are prone to warping.

The cheapest of all real-wood options is a veneered floor. These consist of a thin layer of wood glued to a manufactured board and are supplied ready finished with a plasticized protective coating. If they become worn or damaged, they cannot be refinished.

Woodblock floors are very decorative. Traditional parquet comes in a number of configurations, from the familiar brick shapes arranged in herringbone or basketweave fashion to panels composed of geometric shapes like a wooden patchwork square. Wood mosaic blocks look like parquet in miniature, consisting of narrow strips of wood bonded onto a backing to form a wood tile. Much less expensive than real parquet, they are very easy to lay. End-grain woodblocks have an unusual and distinctive appearance and are very durable indeed.

Wood can be finished in a number of ways. Clear seals in a matt or satin finish enhance the colour of the wood slightly, but otherwise give a natural look. Wood stains come in a range of timber shades as well as some brighter colours and permanently alter the colour of the wood. Paint gives floors a solid coloured finish and covers marks and stains. Purpose-made floor paints are more durable than ordinary gloss or eggshell, but will eventually wear in doorways and other high-traffic areas. Repainting provides a quick and easy solution.

opposite **The parquet floor that extends across the living area of this apartment is a legacy of the old school from which it was converted. Too worn and damaged for repolishing, it was painted with three coats of Farrow & Ball floor paint in off-black Railings to give a very high-gloss finish.**
above left **It takes courage to choose bright red as an all-over floor colour but in this living room it enlivens a predominantly neutral scheme. Red floor paints, ranging from terracotta through to scarlet, are available from specialist makers.**
above centre **Although the first impression is of colour, painted wood floors have texture, too, as the shiny finish highlights the contours of the grain.**
above right **Several coats of varnish have deepened the colour sheen of this dark wood floor and raised its surface to produce an effect similar to Chinese lacquer. Such a dramatic floor works best in a disciplined, architectural interior.**

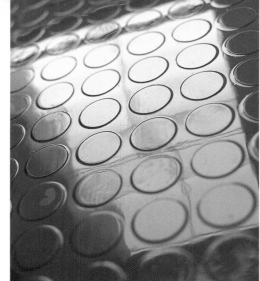

right and below right **Rubber is one of the most durable floor coverings for busy areas and regular polishing will maintain its good looks. Tiles come in various textures to give a slip-resistant surface. As well as the familiar stud pattern, there is a choice of grid, basketweave, ribbed and all-over designs.**

far right **The brilliant blue studded tiles specified for this** colourful kitchen are Omega in Bleu Paon by Dalsouple.

opposite **Modern materials cover every surface in this kitchen with a glossy poured epoxy floor. Plain white may not seem a practical choice for a busy kitchen but poured flooring is self-levelling and perfectly smooth, so is easy to mop, and the pale reflective surface lends a light, airy atmosphere.**

sheet & soft tiling

Rubber, vinyl and linoleum – long regarded as functional floorings – are now emerging from the kitchen to occupy new areas of the home. Chosen primarily for their durability and ease of care, these workhorse materials have an industrial aesthetic that makes them a popular choice for modern domestic interiors.

Smooth, resilient and quiet, sheet flooring and soft tiling are the ultimate coverings for busy areas. They are warm and comfortable to stand on, so a good choice for kitchens, where you spend a lot of time on your feet, and have an ease of care fitting to family life.

Price reflects durability. Treated with respect, the more expensive materials like linoleum, rubber and high-quality vinyl will last for a decade or more. Cheaper vinyl and vinyl-faced cork tiles have a shorter life but allow you to treat the floor as another element in a decorative scheme that can be changed without too great an outlay. Rubber is usually sold in tile form with a smooth or textured surface, in plain colours or patterns. Vinyl flooring comes in sheet or tile form and is more often patterned than plain. The patterns

frequently simulate traditional materials such as wood, brick and tile, but abstract modern designs are starting to appear. Linoleum, a natural material made from linseed oil and wood flour, comes in continuous sheets or as tiles, in a huge range of plain or marbled colours. Where pattern is required, marquetry-like motifs and borders may be inset into the plain ground. Leather, a relative newcomer to the league of smooth flooring, is the wild card here. Far from utilitarian, it is expensive and luxurious, and although it wears well it will stain and scratch if not treated with care.

above left **Once the utilitarian floor covering of kitchens and hospital corridors, linoleum has undergone a change of image. Available in a palette of marbled and plain colours it can be inlaid with borders and motifs in standard or bespoke designs.**
above **Subtle variations in colour are part of the charm of leather floor tiles. Their warm tones naturally complement modern and traditional furnishings.**
near left **Leather is one of the most sophisticated of floor coverings and, because it is warm and slightly giving to the touch, is sensually appropriate for a contemporary bedroom. These tiles are from Bill Amberg.**
far left **Inlaid designs elevate linoleum from utility to designer status. A range of ready-cut inset motifs and borders is available in Marmoleum by Forbo, or individual designs can be cut by a specialist installer.**

opposite, above left **Smooth, shiny and bright, rubber flooring makes a colourful impact in a bathroom. It is completely waterproof but tends to be slippery when wet, so always use a bathmat.**
opposite, above right **An all-white bathroom may be the classic choice but these brilliant rubber tiles by Dalsouple ensure good taste is not taken too seriously.**
opposite, below left **Slip-resistant textured vinyl is laid like a carpet down this flight of steps bringing a splash of colour to a modern interior. Unlike cushioned vinyl, which is soft underfoot, textured sheet vinyl is very durable and available in a wide range of plain colours.**
opposite, below right **Rubber has a well-earned reputation as functional flooring. It now comes in such a choice of colours, as well as marbled and flecked designs, that, increasingly, it is valued for its decorative qualities.**

natural fibres & carpets

In rooms where comfort is the priority, soft flooring has never gone out of style. Warm and quiet underfoot, it envelops a room with a sense of luxury.

Soft flooring has a place in every home: in the bedroom it offers a sensual surface for bare feet; it cushions stairs and hallways against noise; and it provides a link for soft furnishings in the living room. Fitted carpet was once the universal choice, but now the field encompasses natural-fibre floor coverings, rugs and runners. Of these, carpet offers the greatest choice of colour, pattern and texture and comes in a variety of qualities to suit different levels of wear. Plain broadloom is an enduring classic but neutral-toned cut-and-loop pile carpets and striped flat-weaves also have a strong following. If the fitted carpet has suffered from the vogue for hard floors, rugs have benefited. They provide a soft surface just where it is needed – by the bed, in front of the fire – and can add colour to a neutral scheme.

Natural-fibre flooring such as coir, sisal and jute is usually fitted wall to wall. It comes in a range of natural colours and textured weaves that complement both contemporary and country-style furniture.

above far left **New to the ever-lengthening list of plant fibres used to make natural flooring, abaca is a product of the banana family. Softer and smoother-textured than most, with a beautiful silvery colour, it is very durable and produces a satisfyingly chunky weave. Abaca rugs are available from Roger Oates Design.**

above centre left **A graphic relief border carved into a thick pile rug by Christine Vanderhurd adds decoration without introducing another colour to the scheme.**

above centre top **The natural colour of this herringbone coir flooring has an affinity with the rich vegetable-dyed colours of the kelim that lies over it.**

above centre below **Made from rectangles of wool felt joined with blanket-stitched seams, this Tapis rug designed by Roger Oates in low-key colours makes**

an unusual centrepiece for a contemporary room.

above centre right **Natural flooring comes in a range of neutral tones and weaves. Here, rich brown bouclé sisal runs through from the lobby to the bedroom with a rough-hewn granite kerbstone step marking the different level with a change of texture. Kerbstones are available from architectural salvage dealers.**

above far right **The loop-and-pile grid pattern of this cream Target carpet by Stark Carpets has a crisp regularity that makes a suitably disciplined background for contemporary furniture.**

left **Bespoke carpets – dyed, woven, inlaid or carved to order – are available for those with specific requirements. Borders are often incorporated into fitted carpets to emphasize the shape of a room, but this carpet, designed by Helen Yardley, has**

a sinuous 'pathway' pattern of contrasting colour inset to lead the way through a gently curving entrance hall.

right **Texture affects the way colour is perceived, and in this monochromatic carpet by Christine Vanderhurd, the discs of longer pile appear a shade darker than their close-cropped surroundings. Stud designs are common in utilitarian rubber flooring, so the same device interpreted in a much more luxurious material adds a note of elegant humour to a contemporary interior.**

below right **Modern rugs, like this one by Christopher Farr, are valued as works of art and can be the key to the colour and style of a room. Placed at the centre of a seating arrangement, they become a natural focus and receive as much attention as they would hung on the wall.**

WALLS & CEILINGS

WALLS AND CEILINGS ARE WHAT SEPARATE US FROM THE OUTSIDE WORLD. THEY ENCLOSE AND

DIVIDE OUR HOMES, MARKING OUT SHARED AND PRIVATE TERRITORY. MOST ARE SOLID, PROVIDING

A VISUAL AS WELL AS PHYSICAL DIVISION, BUT SLIDING PARTITIONS AND TRANSPARENT PANELS

MAKE AN INTERIOR LAYOUT MORE FLUID AND FLEXIBLE. USUALLY, SOLID SURFACES ARE DECORATED

WITH PAPER, FABRIC OR PAINT, BUT TEXTURAL MATERIALS – WOOD, STONE, BRICK AND CONCRETE

– CAN CREATE A SENSE OF PERMANENCE AND A RICHLY NEUTRAL BACKGROUND.

flexible space

Walls and ceilings define the spaces we live in, separating areas for different activities and allowing privacy where needed, but their solidity and permanence can sometimes be limiting. Employing translucent materials or moveable partitions brings greater versatility.

above **The sliding panels across one end of this kitchen can be opened to flood the room with daylight from the windows opposite or closed to conceal the clutter of cooking.**

above right **In a room with a high ceiling, a sleeping platform suspended from the rafters extends the living space vertically without losing the sense of openness at ground level. Stairs rising to the platform, and their flanking wall, partially separate the study and kitchen areas but, because the wall stops short of the ceiling, light from the skylight floods the whole space.**

left **Subterranean rooms are, by definition, dark, but the basement level of this apartment in a former printworks has been opened up to daylight by enlarging the stairwell and constructing a wall of glass bricks between the bedroom and stairway. The Solaris bricks are ribbed to give privacy while allowing light through.**

Solid walls are necessary to support the structure of our homes, but perhaps we do not need as many as we think. Most internal partitions are there for demarcation, to separate conflicting activities, give privacy or define territory. They help reduce the transmission of sound from one living space to another and they provide a background against which to arrange furniture. However, they also block the passage of light and are sometimes more confining than we would like. Open-plan spaces, having few visual anchors, screens or boundaries, present different challenges, requiring imaginative arrangement of furniture and possessions, tidiness and, in a family home, harmony and cooperation.

Between these extremes, however, there are opportunities for devising a more flexible interior that puts space to good use and can be adapted to changing demands. Moveable walls are an effective way to alter space for aesthetic or practical reasons. They neatly negotiate the limitations imposed by conventional walls by allowing the shape and character of a room to be changed without recourse to builders. In winter, spaces can be made smaller and more snug; in summer, the partitions open up to give an expansive, airy feel. Kitchens, dining rooms, studies or hallways can be screened off when contained spaces are required and opened up for extra space and a more convivial atmosphere. Such partitions can be as simple and temporary as a freestanding screen or a more permanent arrangement of folding doors or sliding panels.

Walls made from glass or other translucent materials may not physically enlarge a space but, by allowing light to pass into gloomy rooms, stairwells and basements from the windows in adjoining rooms, they make more use of the existing area and give a feeling of openness. The ceiling presents another opportunity to open up space and, where there is no loft above, a large skylight will bathe the room beneath it in light, give an enhanced feeling of space and, after dark, a stunning view of the night sky.

far left top and centre **Glass bricks form one side of this shower enclosure allowing light from the bathroom to pass through. Textured rather than clear bricks are used to camouflage the inevitable splash marks.**
far left below **A glass roof ensures this living area is light and bright all year round, and the hard shadows produced on sunny days endow the architecture with a sculptural quality. Glazed roofs must be made from toughened (laminated) glass for safety and fitted with easily operated opening devices for comfort.**
left **The bottom half of this wall is made from obscured glass bricks for privacy. The clear glass above offers a view of the trees, which provide shelter in summer and uninterrupted daylight in winter.**

right **In some situations, absolute transparency can be confusing and potentially hazardous. Here clear glass bricks allow views through the space, but the grid of joints between them indicates the presence of a wall.**
centre right **Translucent glass panels enclose an area of privacy within an open-plan space without greatly reducing the natural light into the adjacent passageway.**
below, left and right **The wall beside this bath is made from Privalite electro-polarizing glass, which contains an interlay that changes from clear to opaque when the power is turned on. Expensive but effective, the glass can be left clear to give a feeling of space in the bathroom or switched on when privacy is required.**

glass

Glass blurs the boundaries of any living space, bringing the outside in or allowing light to spill from room to room.

The brilliance, clarity and translucence of glass makes it a favourite material for modern interiors, where it enhances light and creates a feeling of spaciousness. Glass walls come in the form of bricks or panels and may be textured to obscure the view without sacrificing light. For those who need transparency and privacy at different times, there is electrically controlled glass that can be switched from clear to cloudy.

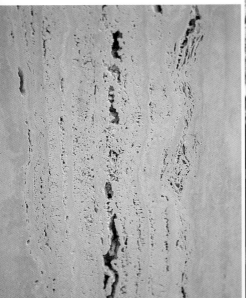

stone, concrete, brick & plaster

On the inside, the hard materials that form the fabric of a building are usually hidden from view, but when exposed, the most familiar of these can take on a decorative value in their own right.

While these hard surfaces, more usually concealed under layers of paint and wallpaper, undoubtedly add character and texture to a room, they are cold surfaces and need the contrast of warmer materials – in the form of furniture, fabrics or other wall surfaces – to create a positive balance.

Stone, concrete, brick and plaster each have a distinct personality, and they seem to divide conveniently into traditional and modern styles; but typecasting is dangerous. Of the four, concrete, a utilitarian material with industrial associations, is more likely to fit its style profile, being most suited to a stripped-back modern interior in a large urban space. The others have more chameleon-like qualities.

above left **The natural fissures that occur in creamy travertine marble give the stone texture and sophistication. It is available as wall panels from marble suppliers.**
above right **The walls of this converted industrial building in the north of England are built from the local gritstone and have been repointed but are** otherwise untreated. **The stainless-steel handrail and plate-steel staircase are stylistically appropriate.**
right **This wall has been stripped back to reveal the texture and mellow colour of the bare brick. Old bricks are invariably dusty, but a broad dado of recycled timbers at the right height will protect passers-by from contact with the surface.**

left **The diagonal beams of this concrete ceiling were left exposed to show its structure and bear witness to the building's industrial origins. The surface was sealed against dust with PVA adhesive, diluted to a consistency that could be completely absorbed so as not to alter the appearance of the concrete.**

opposite, above left **This fireplace wall is built from Idaho quartzite honey ledgestone, which is indigenous to the locality. Laid in a random ashlar pattern with the grout joints raked deep, the arrangement of stones enhances the horizontal lines of the house.**

opposite, above right **The wall and ceiling here are lined with panels of cementitious fibreboard screwed to a wood and steel frame. Revealing elements of the building that are usually unseen gives the interior a raw, unrefined quality.**

opposite, below right **Exposing a brick wall is not simply a matter of hacking away the old plaster. To remove surface dirt, the brickwork should be sand- or grit-blasted – a treatment which, in the case of this wall, softened the colour to a warm honey tone.**

opposite, below centre **Brickwork that is intended to be seen has an entirely different character to the kind that has been stripped of its plaster. Bright, regular and well defined, it can play a leading role in a contemporary scheme alongside other well-groomed building materials such as concrete and timber.**

opposite, below left **This three-dimensional partition contains a shower and handbasin within its organic shape. A conventional stud construction was covered with flexible sheet fibreglass (instead of rigid plasterboard) to form the smoothly curved ends. Its exterior is finished with Armourcoat Spatulata, a decorative, lightly textured finish that resembles Venetian plaster.**

Stone can be stately, elegant, rustic or modern. Think of the perfectly dressed stone walls in the hallway of a Georgian townhouse and compare them with highly finished travertine in a modern bathroom, the rugged granite blocks of a rustic cottage or evenly hewn stones used in a contemporary country home in the mountains. All are stone but, in style and presentation, are quite different.

Brick is equally versatile. The mellow tones and matt, powdery texture of age-worn brick makes it a sympathetic material for both traditional interiors and modern converted industrial spaces, while the bright, uniform colour and regular shapes of new brick have a sleekness that blends well with other well-groomed contemporary surfaces like polished concrete and oiled hardwood.

Plaster is probably the latest material to be recognized for its decorative potential, but where it is left bare it is rarely in its natural form. The new decorative plasterwork is more often a surface coating applied by specialists then polished, textured or tinted to achieve finishes of considerable sophistication. Polished plaster has a chic, metropolitan look, while textured plaster gives an impression of age – if not antiquity – and, in neutral or warm earthy colours, is an ideal backdrop for antique or modern furniture.

this page, above **Veneers allow the natural grain of rare and exotic woods to be used decoratively over a large area. These fitted wardrobes owe their unusual undulating texture to sapele pomelle, a veneer cut from the root of the sapele – a wood sometimes referred to as African mahogany.**

this page, centre left **Rich brown iroko planks fitted horizontally to clad an entire wall are juxtaposed with a clear glass balustrade. The choice of simple, if expensive, materials and the lack of any embellishment create an elegant background for classic contemporary furniture.**

this page, centre right **Fine materials like this burr-oak veneer are unusual in a kitchen, but the quality of the cabinetry forges a unity between this room and the adjoining, similarly luxurious dining room.**

this page, below **Wood panelling need not restrict your colour scheme. Paint is a quick, simple and inexpensive way to change the look of the room without losing its intrinsic character.**

opposite, above left **In this converted oast house, built for the purpose of** drying hops, the original ceiling **would have been slatted to allow heat to rise. The new slatted softwood ceiling, modelled on the old, has been stained to mimic the colour of heat-darkened timbers.**

opposite, above right **This wooden ceiling is unusual in that the timbers appear to run parallel with the rafters – an effect the architect intended to emphasize the ceiling's direction and drama. In fact, the wood in the ceiling is hemlock panelling, milled to replicate the width of the Douglas fir rafters and attached to the underside of the plywood roof decking which spans the rafters.**

opposite, below left **Plywood may be an inexpensive material but, if skilfully installed, it has visual and practical integrity. Here the boards are perfectly level, edges abutted with joints arranged in a regular staggered-brick pattern. Light reflecting off its golden surface casts a warm and flattering glow over the room.**

opposite, below right **Recycled rafters supporting a steeply pitched roof accentuate its soaring height and add to its character.**

wood

One of the most ancient building materials, timber is warm, tactile and responsive. It contributes greatly to the quality of our lives, bringing colour, pattern and a resinous perfume into our homes.

The clichéd view of wood walls and ceilings concerns oak beams and dark panelling, but wood comes in many varieties and offers unlimited decorative possibilities. In the hands of a craftsman, fine veneers cut from rare and exotic timbers create luxurious interiors in the style of an ocean-going liner, while unremarkable timbers like softwood and plywood, used imaginatively, make interesting surfaces with or without the help of stains, seals and lacquers.

top **A contemporary interpretation of the concept of wood panelling, this veneered wall is figured like the contours on a map, the flowing grain contained by leaving narrow spaces between the panels.**

above **Timber in a traditional setting: this oak partition wall conforms to the post-and-panel method of construction commonly used up to the 17th century, where planks or panels filled the spaces between timber studs. The heavy central ceiling beam is one of the main supports for the building's upper storey.**

right **Commonly used in early California Modern architecture, indigenous redwood, cut in broad 30 cm tongue-and-groove panels, clads the walls of this house. It has physical and visual warmth and, used indoors and out, helps blend the building with its natural surroundings.**

this page, top **Sometimes the only economical way to deal with a crumbling ceiling is to cover it up. In this hallway, a virtue has been made of necessity by installing a decorative false ceiling. Painted dark red, it is strengthened by narrow beams in dark green to match the door frames, while rounded corner pieces complete the faux-gothic effect.**

this page, centre **The division of walls into frieze, field and dado was a classically inspired Georgian formula for decorating. Here the dado, including the chair rail and skirting board, is painted white in sparkling contrast with the deep red above.**

this page, below **Panelled walls denote tradition and formality, emphasize symmetry and, in a large room, break up expanses of wall.**

opposite, top left and centre **This fine wood panelling, painted a light putty colour (OW17 by Papers and Paints), is an original feature of this 19th-century house. The lower part is relatively simple but the deep carved frieze is in a typically Aesthetic style.**

opposite, top right **This ceiling in the same house has carved wood cross-ribs in the vernacular style. The pendant light by 20th-century designer Serge Mouille is an unlikely but successful flourish.**

opposite, centre left **First conceived to protect walls from being marked by furniture, wood-panelled dados now serve to improve the proportions of a room and give a sense of character and permanence.**

opposite, below left **Modern décor and traditional architecture can mix provided each is awarded due respect. Here, no attempt is made to disguise the Victorian plasterwork ceiling – rather it is accentuated by painting the moulding in a stronger colour.**

opposite, below right **Tongue-and-groove wainscoting is a serviceable wall treatment most often seen in country kitchens and other hard-working rooms. Here, newly installed tongue-and-groove lines the staircase leading to the basement kitchen of a Regency townhouse. An alcove set into the curved wall is a quirky touch.**

decorative details

Plain, smooth walls and ceilings are blank canvases inviting decoration, and there are limitless ways to embellish them. Surface decoration adds colour and pattern, but plasterwork and panelling adds a third dimension and a sense of permanence.

People have embellished the walls of their homes from the earliest times and it is an urge that evolution and civilization have never dimmed. A traditional way to decorate – and insulate – walls is with timber panelling. The 18th-century fashion for classical architecture led to a formula for positioning the horizontal panel mouldings to correspond with the proportions of the classical column. So, the skirting board represented the column base, the dado or chair rail the pedestal, and the cornice the entablature. This formula survived and, though it is unusual to find rooms with full traditional timber panelling, a wood-panelled dado or at least a dado rail and skirting is a familiar feature. The type of wood panelling found in period houses varies in quality and extravagance of design depending on the status of the room. Below stairs, tongue-and-groove wainscoting was the norm, but much more extravagant panelling can be found in rooms used for entertaining. In older buildings, ceilings, too, are embellished. Usually the decoration is plasterwork which is moulded in complex and elaborate designs, but elsewhere, beams and cross-members form a rectangular grid across the surface.

Plain walls and ceilings are most often decorated with paint or wallpaper in styles that change with fashion. Currently matt paint, the flatter the better, is in vogue, but in past decades satin and gloss finishes have had their moments. Specialist paint finishes are favoured by some as a way of adding pattern and texture to paintwork or producing faux finishes that mimic stone, marble or another natural

left and top left **Leather panels, suspended from a ceiling-mounted track, form an effective partition. Made in the same way as a vertical louvred blind and operated by similar fittings, the overlapping leather vanes appear as a solid partition but are slightly tilted to allow some light through while visually dividing the space. The panels were designed by Filer & Cox.**

above centre, left and right **This wall, pierced with angular recesses in which to display beautifully shaped vessels, was built across an alcove to give the room a square, streamlined plan. The recesses are painted in neutral shades of grey, taupe and chocolate brown and lit from within.**

above right **The visible fibres in this Indian parchment paper from Bilhuber Basics, and the fact that it is hung in panels with visible joints instead of conventional drops, give a subtle texture that makes it difficult to discern whether it is indeed paper or some sophisticated stone finish.**

right **Op-art wallpaper designs need to be seen in their entirety to fully appreciate the illusory effect. This slightly three-dimensional paper is vintage, but similar designs can be found in new ranges.**

far right, above and below **A discreet painted dado has been created by contrasting matt and reflective finishes. Set higher than usual at shoulder height, the dado has a stylized wave edge separating the pearlescent glaze below and the matt paint above.**

material. Glazes add pearly, metallic or sparkling finishes to flat colour to produce playful effects that are, tantalizingly, only apparent when they catch the light.

Wallpapers are an easy way to introduce colour and pattern to a room. As well as thousands of printed designs, there are many interesting textured papers to choose from. Embossed papers were once the most common type and are still widely available in traditional and abstract designs, but blown vinyl, a heat-expanded plastic material applied to the surface, provides the relief pattern on many modern papers. Random-textured papers have taken time to shrug off the downmarket legacy of woodchip, but the newest ethnic or handmade-look papers are glamorous and sophisticated. Sometimes these come in small sheets, like wrapping paper, but accurately hung, with the joins staggered, the result can resemble ashlar stonework.

STAIRCASES

THE STAIRCASE COULD BE SEEN SIMPLY AS A FUNCTIONAL STRUCTURE, BUT BECAUSE IT OCCUPIES

SUCH A PROMINENT AND CENTRAL POSITION IN THE HOUSE, IT IS A MAJOR ARCHITECTURAL

FEATURE. IN TRADITIONAL HOUSES, THE STAIRCASE CAN BE AN ACCURATE INDICATOR OF PERIOD,

BUT IN CONTEMPORARY BUILDINGS, NO SUCH RULES APPLY AND IT CAN BE ENCLOSED IN A

STAIRWELL OR OPEN PLAN, STRAIGHT OR SPIRAL, AND MADE FROM VIRTUALLY ANY MATERIAL

THAT IS SAFE AND STRONG ENOUGH FOR THE PURPOSE.

spatial flow

There's an argument for nominating the staircase as the focus of the home. It is often the first thing you see when you enter the house; it occupies a central position, and it connects every level. The first flight of a staircase is invariably the most impressive as it is a key feature of the entrance hall and its style, whether traditional or modern, can set the tone for the design of the rest of the house.

The staircase is not just a functional structure giving access to the different floors in a house, it is also an important design feature right at its heart and exerts a powerful influence over the areas surrounding it. Traditional staircases made from wood are bulky and occupy a large amount of space. The best of them are beautifully constructed with carved or turned newel posts, sweeping handrails and slow curves that carry the eye upwards. The worst are narrow, ill lit, sharply angled and poorly positioned.

Replacing a less-than-lovely staircase for something more aesthetically pleasing can improve an interior dramatically by making better use of space and by reducing the substance of the staircase to allow more light to pass through. However, the project will be expensive and disruptive and should not be undertaken without professional help and a clear set of objectives. Listed-building owners will need listed-building consent to carry out major changes of this kind and anyone thinking of installing a new staircase must be aware of

above **This centrally positioned staircase is designed as an atrium, naturally lit from a large skylight above and enclosed by glass walls so light passes into the surrounding rooms.**
right **A conventional staircase made from glass gives the very unconventional effect of a light well cutting through all levels of a house.**
opposite **In a spacious loft apartment, a sinuous modern staircase curves around the architecture. It is a dramatic feature, but because of its light frame, does not dominate.**

regulations which stipulate requirements for the pitch of the stairs, the amount of headroom and the design of the banisters.

If your main aim is to reduce the amount of space taken up by the staircase, a spiral design is a possible solution, but bear in mind that it will be difficult to carry large pieces of furniture up and down it, and you will lose much of your useable understairs space. Custom-made spirals are often dramatically sculptural and would have a strong presence in an entrance hall, but those bought from standard ranges are perhaps better suited for linking upper storeys. If your hope is to make better use of the surrounding space in the hall or landing, the staircase may be repositioned to facilitate this,

but if it is important to create a more contemporary look and a sense of space at the centre of your home, a staircase with an open construction, flooded with natural light, is the answer.

One of the most successful ways of drawing light into a staircase is to install a large skylight directly above it. If the staircase has a sufficiently fine framework and is built from translucent materials, the light will pass unhindered through the stairwell making the whole house seem brighter and more spacious. For a project like this, the likelihood is that the staircase will have to be custom-made, but by working closely with an architect or designer the result will be a unique centrepiece to your home.

right **In this house, a contemporary interpretation of the 1930s Moderne style, the staircase typically rises from the living area to open up the space. Open treads and a geometric metal-and-glass balustrade add to the feeling of spaciousness and the effect is enhanced by daylight streaming down from the rooflight overhead.**

below **Curved walls, exposed, grey-painted metalwork and porthole lights give this open-plan interior a nautical atmosphere which is added to by the spiral staircase leading to an open, deck-like landing. Made from a combination of silvery grey metal and light timber, the stairs seem more an integral part of the structure than simply a means of moving from one level to another.**

opposite, left and right **Winding around the perimeter of a sky-lit atrium at the centre of a tall, narrow townhouse, this staircase is a bright space in daylight hours. The glass walls separating the staircase from the surrounding rooms are translucent where privacy is needed and clear where a feeling of space is the priority, but the result is always the same – to double the volume of light flowing through the interior.**

right, above and below **It is hard to believe that this imposing staircase at the heart of an early-19th-century townhouse is less than ten years old. Made to order, it fits the house perfectly, following the austerely elegant late Georgian style of plain square-section balusters set two to a tread with a sinuous, slim mahogany handrail. Winding through the heart of the house, it sweeps in generous curves from the centre of the ground floor to the upper levels and down around a wide stairwell to the basement, encouraging the free flow of light and activity.**

opposite, left **A straight flight of wooden steps may be the most functional of staircases but this one, made from beautifully grained timber, demonstrates how quality of materials and manufacture can elevate a plain design to classic status. Most stairs form the focus of an entrance hall, but in this house where the steep downward slope of the site makes it more practical to site the bedrooms on a lower level than the living area, the staircase leading to them is more discreet.**

opposite, right **A staircase across the centre of a studio apartment may seem like an inefficient use of space, but here, with a short flanking wall, it forms a division between the kitchen and office. The understairs cavity, accessed from the kitchen side, provides housing for appliances. In this predominantly white space, hard maple, a pale and durable wood, faces the treads and risers, bringing definition to the shape of the staircase.**

below left **Open-tread timber steps cantilevered from a wood-panelled wall recede into their background. The open ends of the steps are linked in pairs by chrome bolts which also serve to warn of the projecting edges.**

below right **In an apartment divided into interlocking spaces, this enclosed staircase leads to a mezzanine library at one end of the tall living room. Pavement lights set into the staircase wall allow light from an entrance hall, tucked under the mezzanine, to illuminate the stairs.**

wooden stairs

Traditional stairs are constructed almost entirely from timber, from the unseen structural parts to the carved decoration, but modern staircases made primarily from harder materials often use wooden handrails and treads to add a warm and tactile element.

Wood is probably the ideal material for a staircase. In construction, it is strong and easy to work; decoratively, it is sympathetic and versatile. It lends itself to traditional and modern styles and can be stained, polished, painted or carpeted when a new look is required. Traditional stairs are likely to be more substantial, with rounded stair nosings,

turned balusters and carved newel posts. Modern wooden stairs are pared-down and may consist of nothing more than a series of open treads cantilevered from a wall or wooden facings covering a flight of concrete steps. Where traditional stairs rely on decorative detailing, modern ones let the colour and grain of the wood speak for itself.

glass & metal

For some, climbing a glass staircase is like taking a step into the unknown, but what transparent stairs lack in visual substance they more than make up for in glamour. Seen in fashionable restaurants and stylish office buildings, glass is quickly being accepted as a material for stairs in innovative domestic interiors. Metal stairs, too, are making the move from public to private spaces. Valued for its strength without bulk, metal has become the material of choice for designers of light, open staircases.

Conventional staircases are large, solid structures that occupy considerable space at the centre of a house, blocking the flow of light from the front to the back of the building. Open-tread stairs and fine balusters, in particular the lightness of metal structures, allow some light to penetrate the mass, but transparent and reflective glass stairs allow the free passage of light throughout the space.

Glass – brittle, delicate, easily broken – may seem an unsuitable material for stairs, but put aside thoughts of fragile windowpanes and wineglasses and consider instead the resilient glass of car windscreens and shopfronts. The glass used for stair treads is composed of two or three layers laminated together. The total thickness depends on the size of the tread and the weight it is expected to carry, but in a domestic staircase 32–50 mm is the norm. The glass may be water-clear, coloured or textured and, for safety, should be etched to prevent the surface being too slippery. An alternative material is acrylic. It is virtually identical in appearance to clear glass but easier to work with as it can be cut, machined and drilled into without breaking. Its disadvantages are that the surface will scratch and, as the material is flammable, it may not be used for a staircase that will be an escape route in a fire.

Metal stairs, straight or spiral, can be made with a structure so fine that light appears to pass through unobstructed, an effect that is enhanced if the metal used is polished. Open treads with pierced surfaces combine with balustrades filled with clear glass or acrylic panels, wire mesh or tension wires to increase the ratio of space to structure and give a greater impression of openness without losing any sense of security for those using the stairs.

opposite, above A narrow, enclosed staircase always has the makings of a dark and gloomy place reliant on artificial light, but here, open-tread semi-opaque glass steps allow natural light from above and below to flood through the space. The steps, slightly narrower than the staircase width, are discreetly bolted to the flanking walls, giving them the appearance of floating in space.

opposite, below This staircase, leading from a large, sparsely furnished living space to a gallery bedroom is skeletal in design. Supported on a light framework of black metal, it has slim white laminated treads and a tubular brushed-steel handrail.

this page Architect Alan Power designed this glass staircase contained behind a glass wall as part of a radical remodel of a Georgian terraced house. Extending the full three storeys of the building, the transparent structure allows a skylight at the top to illuminate the open-plan living areas. The toughened glass and acrylic laminated treads rest on stainless-steel shoes, bolted on one side to a steel stringer concealed in the solid party wall and on the other to the triple-laminated glass staircase wall. When the treads are backlit by a sun low in the sky, their front edges glow a luminous blue-green. To help define the steps and make them slip resistant, a dotted border has been etched along the front of each tread.

83

opposite and above left **This sculptural staircase by VX Design and Architecture is a dark and dramatic feature in a light open-plan living space. In reverse of convention, the space below the stairs is open, and the space above is enclosed by a welded rolled-steel plate suspended from the structural steel of the upper floor. The stair treads are made of 15 mm frosted glass held in bottomless welded metal trays. These are fixed to the notched lower edge of the steel plate at one side and to a steel stringer, concealed in the wall, at the other. Although the overall impression is dark, the staircase receives daylight from above and from the underside via the glass treads and open risers.**

above centre top **A large staircase can easily overwhelm a space, but the flowing shape and reflective surfaces of this one** create a stream of light at the centre of a large, open living area. Unusually, the steps are clad with a continuous sheet of aluminium, like a metal carpet, and this is top lit by halogen spotlights to shimmering effect.

above centre bottom **Pierced metal stair treads have enough texture to provide a reassuring grip and the right balance of solidity and openness. This industrial-style staircase, with balustrades made from glass and black mesh, links the living areas in a converted church without restricting the flow of light. When light catches the metal, surrounding surfaces are peppered with pinpricks of light.**

above right **This spiral staircase appears to provide an interior link between a dining room and an upper floor, but it actually gives external access to a roof terrace. The confusion arises because the clear glass stairwell** surrounding the outdoor stairway encroaches into the rectangular interior plan.

centre right **Curving outwards and upwards, this open-tread metal staircase follows the rounded wall of a converted oast house, starting at a gentle climb but rising more steeply towards the top. The simple balustrade repeats the curve but does not detract from it, the space between the handrail and treads being filled unobtrusively with tension wires.**

below right **An open mesh of wire within a tubular metal frame surrounds this stairwell ensuring safety without enclosing or over-shadowing the space. Although the components are relatively inexpensive and the installation simple, the balustrade has a pleasingly functional quality that is not out of place in this domestic setting.**

stone & concrete

Staircases made from stone or concrete have a reassuring solidity underfoot and an unrivalled sense of permanence. Often integral to the design of the building, they are an acute indicator of its style.

Stone or concrete steps can be a permanent reminder of a building's origins. A sweeping stone staircase in an 18th-century house gives an air of grandeur, while concrete steps in a converted commercial building give a clue to its industrial beginnings. In contemporary homes, stone stairs are often more of a decorative statement than an architectural one, with an existing staircase and hallway surfaced with stone tiles or panels. Concrete forms a good base for this treatment, but wooden stairs, provided they are sound and have been levelled with a covering of marine plywood, can be successfully stone clad.

far left **White, precast concrete steps fan out from the central pillar of this spiral stairway, extending the height of the building. The steps end about 100 mm short of the curved stairwell wall, and although there is limited visibility from the staircase to the floors it links, the perimeter gap allows the passage of sound and light from** level to level, making this a true connecting space.

centre, above and below **In this contemporary home, the stairs and landing floor are clad with the same dark 'mussel' limestone, but an impression of contrast is created by the way light strikes the horizontal and vertical surfaces. On the stair risers, the colour and pattern** of the stone is very evident, but on the horizontal surfaces of the treads and landing area, the gleaming polished finish dominates.

above **The white-painted walls, glass brick panels, honey-coloured wooden handrail and slate-clad steps combine in this staircase to create a cool, quiet oasis at the heart of the building.**

HEATING

DESPITE ADVANCES IN HEATING TECHNOLOGY THAT GIVE WARMTH WITHOUT A VISIBLE SOURCE OF HEAT, IN COLDER CLIMES THE HEARTH CONTINUES TO BE THE FOCUS OF ANY COMFORTABLE HOME. OPEN FIREPLACES COME IN AN EVER-WIDENING RANGE TO SUIT TRADITIONAL AND MODERN INTERIORS, WHILE RADIATORS, NO LONGER IN THE BACKGROUND, COME IN PERIOD STYLES AND SCULPTURAL CONTEMPORARY SHAPES.

right **This simple white limestone fireplace, made to order by Stoneworks, is framed with a traditional bolection moulding and has at its centre a simple Amhurst steel grate by Gazco.**

opposite, above left **An essay in understatement, this fire surround is made from Bath stone, just a shade darker than the wall.**

opposite, above right **A pared-down version of a traditional design, this surround is decorated with just three roundels spaced evenly across the frieze. It was made to order by a monumental masons from a finely veined misty white Carrara marble.**

opposite, below left **With its outlined columns and black stars, this limestone surround is influenced by Empire style. Made to order by Chesney's, it is an adaptation of their Thomas Hope surround and contains their Wentworth register grate.**

opposite, below centre **The fireplace and television often compete as a focal position, but when turned off, both leave a blank space at the centre of the room. Here, they are set one above the other – a fan-assisted flue eliminating the need for a conventional chimney. When not in use, a large track-mounted painting slides across to conceal them. The satin stainless-steel fire is designed by MOOArc. The picture slides on a track made by Widney.**

opposite, below right **This chimneypiece designed by IPL Interiors, made from pale limestone, has at its centre contemporary patinated bronze 'Petra' firedogs by Garouste & Bonetti flanking a gas 'log' fire.**

fireplaces

Warming, inviting and visually magnetic, in cooler climates the fireplace is the natural centre of a living room. It is part of the architecture and, whether original to the building or newly installed, its style sets the tone for the room.

Now that homes can be heated cleanly and efficiently from an unseen source, it seems odd that the fireplace still survives, but the warmth, colour and movement of an open fire hold an irresistible attraction that makes it a natural focus. The presence of a fireplace is unsurprising in an older house, where it is a vital part of the architecture and character of a room, but few new homes are built without a hearth in the living room, and modern fireplace design is a growth industry.

Classic fireplaces are composed of a surround or chimneypiece framing the fire opening, a grate where the fuel burns and a hearth to protect the floor from ash and embers. The surround is usually made from marble, natural or reconstituted stone, metal or wood, in a size and style to suit the room. The grate may consist of firedogs to support logs, a fire-basket for logs or solid fuel, or a register grate – a unit made entirely of metal or with tiled panels which fills the fireplace opening and is designed for the efficient burning of coal or smokeless fuel. If you want the look of a real fire without the inconvenience of storing fuel and cleaning the grate, fire-baskets and register grates can be fitted with gas-fuelled flame-effect units or less convincing electric models. Readymade

opposite and above **An inset fire built into the chimneybreast fits flush to the wall and occupies no floor space. A focal point, but never intrusive, it is the ultimate minimalist fireplace. Designed by Unique Environments for a contemporary interior, this fire is made from black metal. The fire-bed is composed of matt white pebbles of various sizes which look natural but are actually ceramic. Unlike real stone, the ceramic is resistant to very high temperatures and will not discolour with heat.**

above right **A 'black box' inset fire seems less cavernous thanks to the reflective bronze Japanese paper covering the wall, which shimmers even when the fire is unlit.**

right **An old stone fire surround is an appropriate choice for this basement family room which must once have been the staff quarters of this 19th-century townhouse. Bought from a salvage yard, it was originally much wider than required, but a 'cut-and-shut' operation to remove the excess width from the centre maintained its symmetry.**

fireplaces in modern, classic and traditional styles are widely available. However, if you are after a bespoke design, these can be commissioned from specialist shops or craftsmen, and period pieces can be found in architectural salvage yards.

The newest kind of open fire, designed for contemporary interiors, is the inset or hole-in-the-wall type. Stripped of the inessentials, these have no surround or mantelshelf and are simply a fire opening set in the wall with a conventional fire-basket or a gas-fuelled fire-bed of pebbles, rocks, synthetic logs or ceramic shapes. Unless they are protected by a glass or metal mesh screen at the front, for safety, inset fires should have a projecting hearth on the floor below or as part of the fire itself.

left **Although the hearth itself is small, the magnificent copper hood above it transforms this fireplace into the central feature of an Arts and Crafts interior. Such a distinctive fireplace would have been designed – and preserved – as an integral part of the building, but occasionally salvaged fireplaces are sold by dealers specializing in the style.**

below far left **A chimneypiece that is wider than it is high has a generous, expansive feel. Its proportions are unusual, but the exaggerated width of this fireplace has an elegance in keeping with the understated traditional American interior. The large hearth is amply filled by a pair of typically Federal turned brass-and-iron andirons.**

below near left **The rugged boulder that forms the lintel over this stone fireplace has survived from the remains of the previous house to occupy this site. A similar fireplace could be constructed from roughhewn stone bought direct from the quarry or via a non-monumental stonemason.**

opposite **Part of the original carved wood panelling in an Aesthetic-Movement house, this chimneypiece has been painted a light putty colour to reduce its visual weight without detracting from the carved decoration.**

above left **Commissioned for a house built in the 1940s in the Arts and Crafts style, this craftsman-made repoussé brass surround frames a trapezoid fireplace opening. While the choice of metal leans towards Arts and Crafts, its angular, asymmetrical design shows distinct Modernist influences.**

below left **In its original state, this Victorian fireplace would have had a white marble surround and patterned tiled panels in the register grate. By painting the surround a warm shade of taupe and replacing the** tiles with plain cream ones, the period detail is toned down and the fireplace blends more comfortably with the eclectic style of its surroundings.

centre **A traditional Victorian fireplace assumes a much more exotic image at the centre of a room decorated in red and black. The cast-iron surround could have been shot-blasted to give a dark gunmetal grey finish, but where an opaque, non-metallic black is required, paint is the answer. Touches of gold paint highlight the relief decoration in the fireplace frieze and echo gold** accents elsewhere in the room.

above **There are differing schools of thought about original architectural features. One is that they should be preserved at all costs, the other is that they reflect the fashions of the past and should be altered or replaced when tastes change. A third, more cautious, view is that they can be integrated into a new style of decoration. Here, this cautious approach works successfully as the fireplace, painted the same colour as the wall, is a significant feature but not a dominating one.**

radiators

For decades, few homes have been without central heating, but until recently the choice of radiators was severely limited. Now that is changing, and there are models to suit every taste.

Where once ridged panels hung in the middle of a wall, sometimes even painted to contrast with the surface behind them, now heating is increasingly discreet. Radiators are hidden behind panelling or in a trench, with only a neat grille to indicate their presence. Where they are exposed, radiators are chosen for their inconspicuous styling and ability to blend into surroundings or because their design adds to the overall look of the space they heat.

Radiators must have space around them to allow the heat to circulate, so to a degree they determine the arrangement of furniture in a room. However, they can be made to slot

above far left **Least obtrusive of all radiators, trench heaters, produced by companies such as Jaga, are sunk into the ground and covered with a grille flush to the floor. Because they are so well insulated, any type of flooring can be used around them.**
above centre left **Chosen for its workmanlike appearance and its high heat output in relation to its compact shape, this finned tubular radiator by Gunning Engineering in one of four heating a large studio apartment in a converted industrial building.**
above centre right **Boxed-in radiators look best when they are part of the architecture, and here the radiator cover fills the window alcove. A long grille set into the top of the cabinet allows rising heat to escape, warming the cold area close to the glass.**
above near left **Traditional column radiators assume a contemporary look when they are much taller than they are wide. A number of manufacturers make the columns individually so while there is a range of standard heights, almost any width can be achieved.**
below far left **The designer of this all-white hall chose this Zehnder panel radiator for its low visual input and high heat output. Virtually uncontoured, with its fine horizontal seams casting minimal shadows, the panel seems to disappear into the wall behind.**
below centre **The Zehnder Radiavector is one of the few radiators shallow enough to fit under a window as low as this without obscuring the glass. A double convector radiator, it efficiently counteracts the cooling effect of the uncurtained window.**
below near left **In a bathroom, where space is often limited, a radiator that is part-heater, part-towel rail, like those from the Ecotherm range by Thermic, earns the space it occupies. The wide spaces between rails allow for bulky towels, but some rails must be left uncovered to allow heat into the room.**

above left **Slim and unobtrusive, this panel heater is set into an alcove where its surface is unlikely to come into accidental contact with bare skin. A rail fitted above allows towels to dry quickly and keep warm without blocking heat from the room.**

above Traditional column radiators come in sizes to fit almost any situation. They can even be shaped to fit a curved wall. This wall-mounted example is the Multicolumn by Zehnder, and can be stove enamelled in a range of colours.

left **A radiator cover hides an ugly radiator and integrates it in the room. This painted wood cabinet designed by IPL Interiors has a limestone shelf cut into the window embrasure to give an immaculately tailored fit.**

opposite, above left **If you buy salvaged radiators, make sure they have been refurbished. This**

floor-standing cast-iron radiator has been shot-blasted to clean away the old paint and chemically flushed to remove silt and corrosion from inside.

opposite, above right **A radiator's heat output is related to its surface area, so a long low radiator gives as much warmth as a narrower taller one. This squat column radiator by Clyde Combustions has been fitted with a thick wooden bench to give it a more contemporary look and to help prevent rising heat from escaping through the window.**

opposite, below **It is hard to find the right reclaimed fittings when you want them, so if you see something you like, buy it and wait for an opportunity to use it. These matching short radiators were a salvage-yard impulse buy, but installed side by side they make a stronger visual feature than a single long radiator.**

snugly into restricted spaces – long and low to fit under a large window or tall and slim to fill an alcove or the narrow space between two doors – thus allowing more flexibility. Debate continues about the advisability of positioning radiators under windows. While some heat will be lost through the glass, what is often a chilly part of the room will be made warmer and more usable. In bathrooms, towel radiators with horizontal rails are a practical option as they dry towels while they heat the room.

As radiators are semi-permanent fixtures, it is important to select a design that is compatible with your personal furnishing style and the style of the building. Period-house-dwellers after a traditional look have the choice of buying reproduction column radiators or hunting down suitable vintage ones in salvage yards. Column radiators are usually produced in sections, so can be made to the length required. Modern streamlined panels and sculptural feature radiators are available for contemporary interiors, and models that were designed for use in industrial settings are now available to those who live in converted commercial buildings. New radiators are usually primed and ready for painting, but increasingly they can be supplied with a more durable factory-applied coating in a choice of standard colours or metallic and customized finishes.

stoves

Undoubtedly cleaner and more efficient than an open fire, the workmanlike stove can heat water, supply radiators and boil a kettle, as well as providing direct warmth and a visual focus, whether it is on or off.

Above all, stoves are infinitely versatile. They can stand in the hearth like a conventional fire, flames flickering visibly through the glass-panelled doors, or in the middle of a room radiating controllable heat. They can be powered by solid fuel, wood, oil, gas or electricity and have a predictable heat output measured in kilowatts. Although they still have a rustic image, styles range from basic pot-bellied and box stoves, through matt-black or colourful enamelled traditional designs, to decorative reproduction Art Nouveau styles and extremely stylish contemporary examples.

above **Cylinder stoves are ideal for small spaces like this converted railway carriage as they occupy the minimum of floor space. Although this Summerford model was made only a few years ago it is no longer in production, but similar stoves are available.**

right **A high-output stove with an interior flue produces enough heat to give background warmth for this open-plan house. The Vermont Castings Defiant is similar to this double-door wood-burning stove and comes in coloured enamel finishes as well as matt black.**

opposite, above left **This antique wood-burning stove was designed with safety in mind: a rail at the front prevents logs falling out and clothing from catching the flames.**

opposite, above right **Box stoves are simple fuel burners: basic, inexpensive and sometimes even portable. Stoves similar to this were taken on early polar expeditions and are still used in country cabins and on longboats. This plain design is an antique Shaker stove, but similarly functional models are available new.**

opposite, below left **Stoves are not always rustic or traditional, and many will sit comfortably in a modern setting. The Danish Rais 86 wood-burning stove, designed by Bent Falk in 1970, is a contemporary classic. A wide cylinder with a compartment below the firebox for storing wood and another above it with a soapstone plate for baking, the stove can heat a large living space.**

opposite, below right **Many stove producers have been manufacturing for generations, and although new models are introduced from time to time, the design process is more often one of evolution. This traditional Scandinavian multifuel stove, made by the Danish manufacturer Morsø, is an earlier version of their current Lion Radiant stove.**

STORAGE

WELL-PLANNED STORAGE BRINGS ORDER AND A SENSE OF SPACIOUSNESS TO ANY INTERIOR,

HOWEVER SMALL, LEAVING MORE ROOM TO DISPLAY FAVOURITE THINGS. PURPOSE-MADE UNITS

FOR LIVING ROOMS AND BEDROOMS COME IN CHIC BUT FUNCTIONAL DESIGNS THAT CONTRIBUTE

TO THE STYLE OF THE ROOM, AND FITTED CUPBOARDS, TAILORED TO MAKE EFFICIENT USE OF

LIMITED SPACE, CAN BE SO CLEVERLY CONCEALED THAT YOU BARELY KNOW THEY ARE THERE.

living rooms

Here storage needs to show off and enhance your favourite possessions, while being good-looking in its own right.

The living room is where we gather around us the things we enjoy. It is here we read, listen to music, watch television or spend time with friends and family and it is here, too, that we keep the books, magazines, videos, DVDs, CDs, games, musical instruments and other possessions that are the equipment of relaxation. These things reflect our interests and by displaying them we stamp our personality on the room.

left **Bookshelves tailored to fit under the eaves of an attic room make use of an under-employed space and provide a windowsill to display objects.**

below left **Designed in the 1980s by Vicent Martínez, the Literatura by Punt is a double bookcase with narrow shelves at the front which slide on tracks to reveal the continuous shelves behind.**

below **A wall of shelving is a practical way to provide a great deal of storage. This design by Bataille & ibens is fitted with sliding doors made from white Colorbel colour-enamelled glass by Glaverbel. They cover the lower part and hide the bar, stereo system, television and the entrance to the adjoining laundry room. A wheeled ladder allows access to the higher shelves.**

right **Chosen to house an extensive art library, this Studimo shelving system by Interlübke is arranged here on two levels, the upper level being reached by a separate staircase. The shelves form a regular grid to accept books of any size so the collection can be catalogued without restriction.**

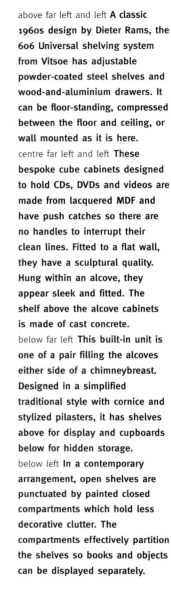

above far left and left **A classic 1960s design by Dieter Rams, the 606 Universal shelving system from Vitsoe has adjustable powder-coated steel shelves and wood-and-aluminium drawers. It can be floor-standing, compressed between the floor and ceiling, or wall mounted as it is here.**

centre far left and left **These bespoke cube cabinets designed to hold CDs, DVDs and videos are made from lacquered MDF and have push catches so there are no handles to interrupt their clean lines. Fitted to a flat wall, they have a sculptural quality. Hung within an alcove, they appear sleek and fitted. The shelf above the alcove cabinets is made of cast concrete.**

below far left **This built-in unit is one of a pair filling the alcoves either side of a chimneybreast. Designed in a simplified traditional style with cornice and stylized pilasters, it has shelves above for display and cupboards below for hidden storage.**

below left **In a contemporary arrangement, open shelves are punctuated by painted closed compartments which hold less decorative clutter. The compartments effectively partition the shelves so books and objects can be displayed separately.**

above **These recessed shelves, tapered to fill the space under the stairs, are plastered and painted to appear as an integral part of the wall. Divided horizontally and vertically, they form niches in which to display favourite objects.**

left **A false wall built across one end of this dining room creates a substantial volume of storage. The space within is divided into two cupboards, and a pair of maple-framed sandblasted glass doors maintain symmetry.**

Different things require different types of storage. Books, especially if they form a substantial library, need sturdy shelving, and many of the best readymade modular systems have become design classics. CDs and DVDs, too, can be packed on shelves, but some individual objects, such as a piece of studio glass or a handmade ceramic bowl, whose prime purpose is to give visual pleasure, need space around them to be seen and appreciated. Where storage must be confined to one area – filling an alcove or covering a wall – shelves can be compartmentalized with vertical partitions to allow books and objects to be displayed together without encroaching on each other's space. In the interest of tidiness or safekeeping, some possessions are best stored in containers and most systems allow for this by incorporating drawers or closed cupboards. Where they do not, baskets or boxes can be placed on open shelves as a simple and inexpensive alternative.

bedrooms

The volume of storage required in a bedroom means that cupboards are as much a part of the décor as they are practical furnishings, making them central to the style of the room. Fitted units are often the best solution, and simple designs will recede to become an integral part of the room and a background for other furniture.

above far left and left **So plain it could be mistaken for wood panelling, this custom-made birch-veneer wardrobe opens to reveal a meticulously planned interior. Rails are fitted in two tiers to make the best use of space, with a separate rail for shirts. The remaining space is devoted to drawers and pigeon-holes. An interior light ensures everything is easy to see.**

left **In the same room, the panelling theme continues with a headboard and integrated nightstands in maple-edged birch veneer. The wall sconces are by Christian Liagre.**

above **Some furniture includes fittings to keep make-up, scarves and accessories in order, but drawer dividers can be bought separately to organize interior space.**

opposite, above left and centre left **The next best thing to a walk-in closet, this capacious wardrobe opens up to give a view of the entire contents. When closed, it blends into its white-painted surroundings.**

opposite, above right **Shallow drawers hold shirts without crushing them, and glass fronts allow you to find the one you want.**

opposite, below left **A filing system for clothes – small drawers keep individual garments immaculate and sloping pigeon-holes store shoes.**

opposite, below right **A sophisticated solution to clothes storage, this oak-lined Cuban mahogany wardrobe wraps around one end of the dressing area off a master bedroom. Slim stainless-steel handles emphasize the height of the doors.**

Clothes need careful storage. They must be easy to find and come out of the wardrobe fresh, unrumpled and ready to wear. They need space to hang freely; folded garments should be stacked, uncrushed, in piles of two or three in shallow drawers or shelves. Shoe racks or pigeon-holes neatly sidestep the confusion of shoes found at the bottom of so many wardrobes, and small drawers (or partitions in larger ones) keep smaller items in order.

work & leisure

Clutter is bad for you. It distracts you while you work and makes you restless when you want to relax. Ruthlessly clearing out possessions is one solution, but there will be things you can't or don't want to dispose of, and for these you need well-organized, good-looking storage.

Two major clutter-creating areas of your home are the office or work space and the viewing and listening area. Technology promised to simplify storage in these areas, as computers, mini discs and DVDs packed more information into a smaller space. In reality, the paperless office is still a distant dream; music and video collections expand to overflow the available space; and housing electronic hardware is complicated by changing formats as hi-fis become smaller, TVs larger and home offices better equipped. Tackle these issues by providing shelves for the things you want to keep in view and cupboards for those you don't.

this page **Where a wall of tall storage might seem to enclose the room, these custom-built cabinets end at shoulder height, leaving space above for displaying pictures. Sliding doors can be opened easily in this confined space. In the upper section, these are made from frosted glass that can be drawn aside to reveal either the television screen or the decorative objects that stand alongside it.**

opposite, above left **Designed to fill the whole wall from floor to ceiling, this fitted storage system contains videos, tapes, discs and all the other paraphernalia of home life behind closed doors, with only a wall-mounted CD player visible. Electronic controls allow the door concealing the television to be opened from the comfort of the sofa.**

opposite, centre left **A narrow aluminium-fronted shelf suspended below wall-hung cupboards contains hi-fi components. Ranged side by side, they appear to occupy less space than they would stacked vertically. The usual untidy trail of cables is eliminated by the use of wireless speakers.**

opposite, below left **Complete in a colourful freestanding unit designed by Christian Biecher, this capsule home office keeps everything within easy reach.**

opposite, above right **When space and budget are limited, a simple DIY solution can work as well as sophisticated purpose-made furniture. Here, a galvanized-steel shelf unit becomes an ad hoc computer desk screened from the rest of the room – but not from the light – by a translucent Perspex™ screen in a dark wood frame.**

opposite, below right **Carefully tailored to house the television, hi-fi, speakers and a Linn system that provides music for the rest of the house, this storage system is built from MDF spray-painted in metallic dark grey lacquer, with door panels of stretched speaker fabric. Designed with an eye to the future, it has enough shelving to accommodate a fast-growing music collection.**

opposite **A row of tall cupboards in a passageway adjoining a kitchen and family room has the capacity to hold everything from crockery to craft materials, leaving the living space uncluttered. Independent but matching, the cupboards have a simplicity of design that does not detract from the vaulted ceiling.**
above left **A wall of bookshelves would not shave more than 30 cm from the width of a hall or landing, so in all but the narrowest spaces, a library hallway is a practical proposition. Here, the book-lined passage houses the overspill from the study beyond and is wide enough to have a seat for browsing in comfort.**
above centre **A similar treatment for a passageway linking two rooms, but this time storage is** behind the closed doors of low cupboards and the shelf space above is lit to give an impression of greater space at eye level.
above right **The smallest and most awkward spaces can be turned into useful storage. Here, a tiny cupboard has been squeezed into the narrow alcove beneath a window and next to a fixed settle. Ending short of the windowsill, its top forms a shelf.**
left **Built at the edge of an open-plan mezzanine bedroom, this painted wardrobe doubles as a screen between the bed and the floor below.**
below left **A series of built-in cupboards rises in tiers to fill a whole wall. Arranged in order of decreasing size, the largest are at floor level to give easy access to bulky items in frequent use, like the baby buggy.**

hallways

The entrance hall may have its own storage needs, but landings and other through routes can provide a permanent home for things that have nowhere else to go.

Passageways and corridors are necessary but largely wasted spaces. They allow you to move around your home without passing from room to room, but most of the time they stand empty. If width allows, one or both walls of a hall or landing may be fitted with shelves or cupboards, and in smaller, awkwardly shaped spaces, an attractive piece of storage furniture will hold your possessions and look good.

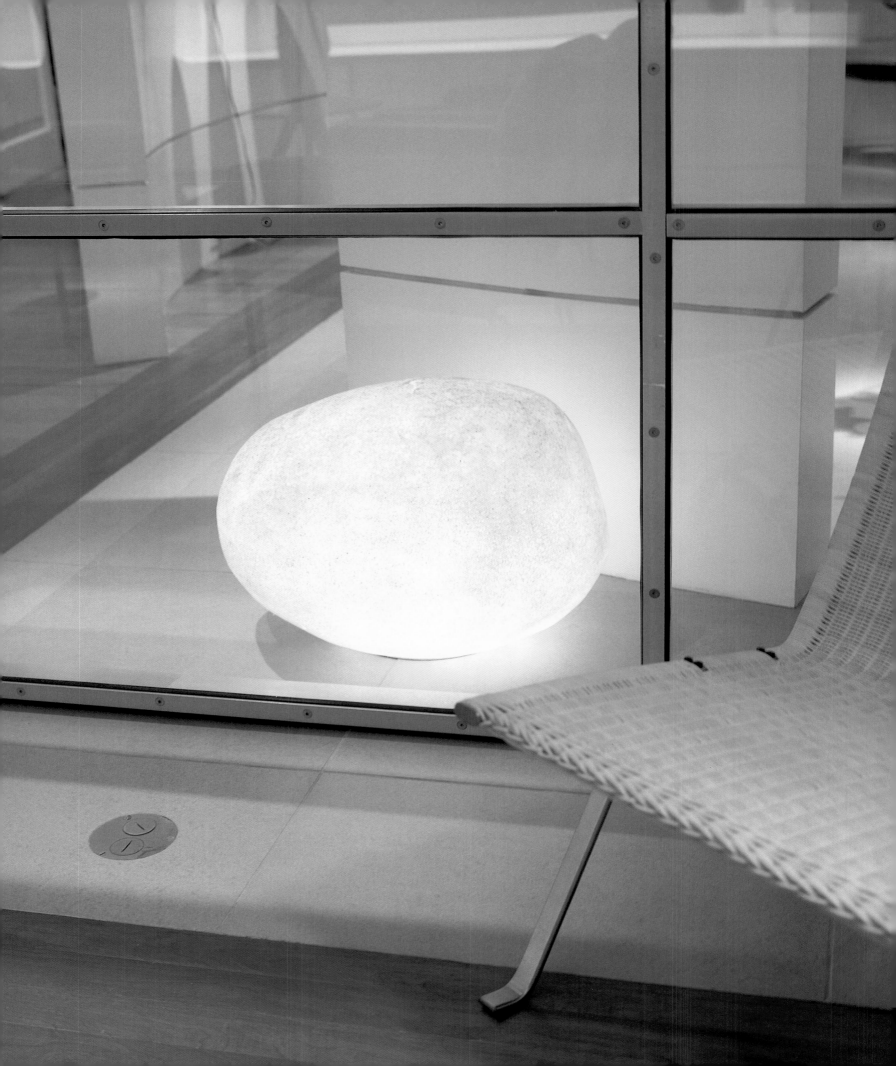

LIGHTING

GOOD LIGHTING BRINGS A ROOM TO LIFE, CREATING ATMOSPHERE, HIGHLIGHTING POINTS OF INTEREST AND ENHANCING THE COLOURS AND TEXTURES OF FURNISHINGS. TO ACHIEVE THE MOST INTERESTING EFFECTS, COMBINE FITTINGS THAT GIVE BRIGHT DIRECT LIGHT, SOFT DIFFUSED ILLUMINATION AND WARM BACKGROUND LIGHT WITH DECORATIVE FREESTANDING LAMPS, THEN ADD DIMMER CONTROLS TO FINE-TUNE THE RESULT.

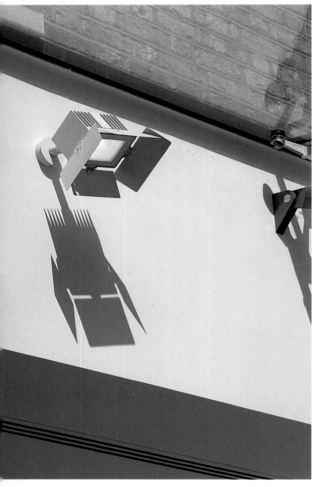

information & decoration

Electric lights replace daylight after dark and supplement it when natural light is insufficient, but the fact that they are necessary is no reason for them to be purely functional. A powerful decorating tool, lighting can enhance or subdue colours, flatter or play down objects and architectural features, and subtly indicate the layout of your space.

Every interior needs general illumination, but it is the additional lighting that, by drawing attention to the features and hazards in our homes, makes them attractive, convenient and safe to live in. Information lighting is one of the most practical examples of lighting for emphasis, and might take the form of an exterior light above the front door or lights recessed into the floor along a windowless hallway. Decorative emphasis is provided in many ways. A spotlight that highlights a piece of furniture, a floodlight that accentuates the size and openness of an interior space, wall lamps that emphasize the texture or colour of a wall, concealed lights that suggest mystery – all play their part in creating visual interest.

top left **Paper, parchment and many natural textiles make excellent materials for lampshades as they conceal the light source while allowing softened, diffused light to pass through. Choose a bulb of not more than 60 watts to avoid scorching the material. This understated but sophisticated wall lamp has a drum shade made from closely woven raffia in a neutral tone that warms the light to a mellow gold.**

above left **Floodlights – normally associated with outdoor lighting – can be used indoors to fill the space with brilliant light, casting shadows that accentuate the contours of the architecture. These Optec tungsten halogen floodlights by Erco have barn-door fittings which can be adjusted to alter** the breadth and direction of the beam. Placed high on the rear wall of a large glass garden room, they add drama after dark.

above centre **Considered lighting design gives emphasis to the solid forms in this kitchen-dining room designed by architect Graham Phillips. Blue fluorescent tubes are concealed above the kitchen cupboards and beneath the counter to wash the ceiling with blue light and make the counter appear to float in space. Tiny halogen spotlights recessed above the kitchen counter drench the surface in clean bright light for cooking, and more recessed spotlights in the ceiling of the dining area form pools of light along the tabletop.**

top right **A series of lights recessed into the wall along a landing indicate direction and provide low-level illumination at night, as well as reassurance for guests who may be unfamiliar with the layout of the house. These SKK 'Walk on me' spotlights, also suitable for outdoors, are waterproof and come in a choice of colours.**

above right **Lights fitted at skirting-board level on a staircase sharpen the contrast between light and shade, making the distinction between treads and risers more defined. These Monsoon low-glare uplights and step lights by John Cullen Lighting fit flush to the surface and may be used on a horizontal or vertical plane.**

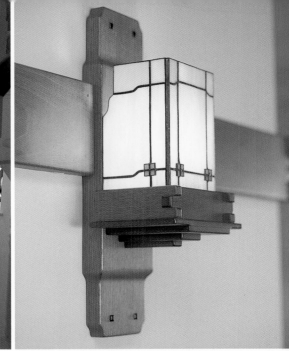

above left **Unlike the original tungsten strip lights, which had a cap at each end to house the electrical connection, modern ones have the connection at the back and can be fitted end to end to give a continuous linear light with no obvious joins. The Philinea light from the Philips Professional range comes in lengths of 500 mm and one metre.**

centre left **Wall lights look good in pairs. Emphasized by duplication, they also bestow importance on the object placed between them. The lamps in this hallway are copies of original American Arts and Crafts designs and flank a table in the same style.**

below left **Designed in the 1950s, the sculptural Tripod lamp by Serge Mouille still looks modern. Using the wall as a diffuser, it washes the surface with light to illuminate the room without glare.**

above centre **Changes to the layout of this house involved the removal of a door at the turn of the stair, leaving a bare landing. To create interest, a panel was installed here. It appears to float unsupported by virtue of concealed lighting which visually distances the panel from the wall behind.**

above right **Unlike ceiling lamps, which often go unnoticed when they are switched off, wall lamps are very visible decorative objects. This distinctive example was handmade by American craftsman Sam Mossaedi for an Arts and Crafts house.**

centre right **Fluorescent strip lighting concealed in a light box behind the mirror directs light downwards to highlight the basin and enhance the colour and texture of the marble.**

below right and opposite **Stairs leading down to a basement are lit for safety and effect by square spotlights recessed low in the wall so the light skims the treads, accentuating the texture of their carpeted surface. Similar spotlights are the Square Skirting Lamps from SKK. Unusually for a basement, the half-landing through the square archway has a rooflight, bringing daylight into this naturally dark space.**

uplighters & downlighters

Uplighters bounce light off the ceiling, which acts as a giant reflector bathing the room in even, diffused light. By contrast, downlighters beam down into the room, flooding the space with bright, direct light.

As sources of ambient light, uplighting and downlighting are usually provided by a number of fittings spaced so their beams overlap one another to give even illumination. Uplighters may be freestanding floor lights or directional wall-mounted fittings. Downlighters are usually recessed into the ceiling and are therefore extremely discreet, but because they shed a vertical beam, have a tendency to leave the walls unlit. This can be overcome by choosing directional fittings that cast light across the surface of the wall.

opposite, above left **An industrial look is achieved by fitting an aluminium spotlight to bare brickwork and running the surface wiring through a metal conduit. The lamp, a Hemisphere spotlight by Box Products, is adjustable, but here it is angled to cast its wide beam downwards.**

opposite, main picture and centre left **Indirect light reflected off the walls or ceiling gives even, glare-free illumination. These aluminium halogen Lingotto lamps, designed by architect Renzo Piano and made by iGuzzini, can be adjusted horizontally and vertically to direct the beam precisely.**

opposite, below left **Used here as an uplighter, the Tolomeo Faretto wall lamp has an adjustable head with a wide beam. Designed by Michele De Lucchi and Giancarlo Fassina for Artemide, it is made from polished and anodized aluminium.**

opposite, below centre **The wedge-shaped Trion uplighter by Erco, mounted high on the wall, directs its beam onto the ceiling to give clean, all-over reflected light.**

opposite, below right **A combination of uplighting and downlighting exaggerates changes in ceiling height along a hallway. The uplighter at the end of the passageway seems to beckon you on to a brighter, loftier, more open space.**

this page, above **Downlighters recessed into the ceiling are angled to form arcs of light on a raspberry-pink wall, while wall-mounted uplighters add contrast between foreground and background.**

this page, below left **The uplighter over this writing table is a terracotta cone held in a wall-mounted wrought-iron hoop designed by Garouste and Bonetti from David Gill. Because the light is directed towards the ceiling, task lighting is required on the desktop.**

this page, below right **A linear halogen bulb set in a fold of metal with a glass lens completing the third side of the triangle forms the sharp Nelson uplighter. It is supplied as a wall-mounted fitting or freestanding lamp by SKK.**

123

tracks & spotlights

Spotlights are the ultimate directional lighting and can be adjusted to highlight objects, pictures, architectural features, surfaces and other areas you wish to accent. Not too distantly related to stage lighting, they produce theatrical effects and add drama to a room. Tracks give spotlights even more flexibility, allowing the light source to be moved anywhere along their length.

Spotlights, by definition, produce a narrow beam of concentrated light and are horizontally and vertically adjustable, allowing them to be targeted accurately. Mains-voltage spotlights are usually fitted with an incandescent reflector lamp, the interior surface of which is silvered except for the top, thus restricting the angle of beam to no more than 30 degrees. Low-voltage spotlights are fitted with a halogen dichroic reflector which is mirrored and faceted to direct light forward and heat backwards, giving a bright, cool light.

The range of spotlight fittings available is extremely varied and includes surface-mounted lights for permanent schemes, floor-standing and clip-on fittings that offer complete flexibility, and track-mounted designs that give flexibility within a fixed system. Styles vary, too, from simple fittings that are little more than lamp holders to sleek designs in polished or colour-coated metal and etched glass, and stylish architectural lights. The latter are often the work of highly regarded designers and architects and offer top performance and a pared-down, industrial style.

Track lighting design has benefited enormously from the development of low-voltage lighting for domestic interiors. Less obtrusive and more versatile than before, it can be mounted on virtually any horizontal or vertical surface, suspended from cables or rods or, in the form of a 'barewire' system consisting of unsheathed low-voltage cables, strung under tension across a room. Some tracks will carry a number of different but compatible fittings, allowing pendants, spotlights, and in the case of suspended tracks, uplighters to share the same power source.

far left **Rather than advertise its industrial origins, this spotlight's enclosed lamp and white finish give it a more domestic look.**
left **A modern alternative to the brass picture light, this low-voltage Electro Track system allows lights to be positioned anywhere along the brushed stainless-steel track and adjusted to light the pictures perfectly.**
opposite, above left and above centre **Sleek and discreet, track lighting can have decorative value in its own right. This system by Optelma has a pair of slim, silvery tramlines that can be fitted to follow a straight line or smooth curves. Different types of lamp – in this case pendant and spot – can be attached anywhere along its length to give a varied lighting scheme.**
opposite, above right **The Gary fitting by SKK is a neat, fixed spotlight consisting simply of a wall bracket and lamp holder for a low-voltage dichroic bulb. A straight handle, seen here to the left of the fitting, can be used to adjust the direction of the beam.**
opposite, centre left **Small and unobtrusive pendant fittings, with translucent shades shielding halogen lamps, hang like tiny globes of white light.**
opposite, below left **This cast-aluminium Pollux halogen spotlight by Erco has an open modular system which, by the addition of coloured or contoured filters projecting abstract images such as rippling water or broken glass, offers opportunities to play with lighting effects.**
opposite, below right **In this formal living room with a strictly monochromatic scheme, spotlights fitted to a track that travels the perimeter of the room are angled to emphasize the shape and texture of furnishings.**

top left **A modern flourish against a traditional panelled ceiling, this metal spiral light, L'Escargot by Serge Mouille from David Gill Gallery, is a fine example of 20th-century design.**

top centre **Another 20th-century classic, the 1968 Flower Pot lamp by Verner Panton has recently been brought back into production by Unique Interieur. Originally designed to hang in the atria or stairwells of large buildings in clusters of twenty and more, this hemispherical lamp has always been used individually in domestic interiors.**

top right **This fine Arts and Crafts lantern is carefully proportioned to fit** a lofty, narrow stairwell. The height of the space is celebrated by the design of the metal lantern, whose tall glass panels reflect the shape of the wall panels, and by the prominent ceiling rose that draws the eye upwards.

above left **Another original Arts and Crafts lamp, custom-made to suit the space it occupies, this metal-and-glass chandelier built by the Mica Lamp Co. throws light upwards to illuminate the beamed ceiling.**

above centre **This Holophane prismatic glass lamp with chromed brass fitting is a 1930s original that sheds a bright but glare-free light. Hector Finch sells** both original Holophane lamps and their own Prism reproduction version.

above right **This classic lamp, the Poulsen PH2/1, designed by Poul Henningsen, has a wide-angled shade to give a broad beam of light. Here it is attached to a custom-made double-angled bracket to allow the position and height to be adjusted.**

opposite, left above and below **Designer David Mullman believes the central light fitting in a room should be luminous and supported by additional light sources to illuminate walls and corners. In this living room the central light is the Archetype pendant by** Boyd Lighting, which has a white fabric shade and satin-nickel stem and canopy. The table in the adjoining dining room is lit by a pair of Reflexion lamps made by Taller Uno. These have a dramatic stepped profile of concentric white cotton cylinders. Each fitting contains one 100-watt lamp and three 60-watt lamps and is controlled by a dimmer switch.

opposite, right **Inexpensive aluminium IKEA lamps have a functional style that suits them perfectly for an informal dining area where, hung as a pair, they have more visual impact and give a wider spread of light.**

pendant lamps

Hanging lights are generally frowned upon by lighting designers, yet few homes are without them. Roundly condemned for giving an unsubtle, all-over light, they are too often left to provide the only illumination in a room. They can, however, be both functional and decorative within a more complex lighting scheme.

The elaborate plasterwork ceiling rose of a period home loses all relevance unless a suitable light fitting is suspended from it, and the chandelier, that mainstay of traditional decoration, has been newly discovered by designers of modern romantic interiors. Likewise, the interest in retro and Scandinavian modern styles has focused attention on the classic lamps of the 20th century, many of which were pendant fittings. Of course, the centre of the ceiling is not the only position for pendant lights and they need not be hung singly. Indeed, they gain from repetition. Hung in pairs over a dining table or in an evenly spaced series along a hallway, they can be as effective and have more visual impact than any downlighter.

task lighting

The lamps we use when we need extra light to work by are known as task lights. Essential for jobs that involve close concentration and attention to detail, they provide a pool of bright but glare-free light and are precisely adjustable to direct light exactly where it is needed.

The term task lighting immediately brings to mind an image of a desk lamp angled over the page or keyboard, and the lamp that forged that image is the Anglepoise. This classic, designed in the 1930s and still available today, stands on a heavily weighted base and swivels, pivots, rotates and tilts with ease and accuracy into stable positions. If the Anglepoise seems to be the definitive task lamp, it has not prevented some of the 20th century's great design minds from attempting to improve on it. Many of the new lamps are less bulky and accept halogen tungsten bulbs – plus points which mean they occupy less space on the desktop and give a cleaner, whiter light.

There are, however, other tasks requiring good light for which an angled desk light is not always the most suitable fitting. In a kitchen, for example, where the cook may be working in his or her own shadow, well focused, fixed illumination over the countertop and hob will light up the working area and improve safety. Good lighting is essential for reading, and in the living room a standard lamp or table lamp set at the right height will provide it. In the bedroom, the best reading lights are adjustable, so here, wall-mounted pivoting or flexible goosenecked fittings, or their tabletop equivalents, will offer the right amount of movement.

opposite **If your taste leans to modern functionalism, the wall-mounted Nelson Flexi by SKK is the perfect bedside lamp. Small and unobtrusive, it has a fully directional flexible stem. The satin-chrome shade is wide angled to give an even spread of light, but opaque so the beam can be directed away from a sleeping partner.**
below left **Designed in the early 1970s by Richard Sapper for Artemide and still in production, the iconic Tizio lamp has the distinction of being the first widely available halogen** tungsten light for the home. Conceived as a desk light, but equally at home in the living room, a tall base is available to convert it into a floor-standing reading lamp.
below centre **Another product of the fertile early 1970s, the 265 designed by Paolo Rizzatto for Arteluce is an extraordinary, elegant fitting, part task light, part wall lamp. Mounted on a swivelling wall bracket, the arm – over two metres in length – is balanced for vertical adjustment, and the head is directional. Here, the** brackets are fixed to the walls of a dining room and the lamps angled to reach over the table.
below right **Unlike most kitchen worktop lighting, concealed behind a baffle, the Homalux light by Homeier is designed to be seen. The translucent lens sheds a bright, diffused light and the chrome frame matches other metal kitchen accessories.**
bottom left **Frank Lloyd Wright created this reading lamp as an integral part of a wide-armed sofa. A freestanding reproduction of this design is made** by the Yamagiwa USA Corp and is available from Strictly Mission.
bottom centre **Proof that good design is timeless, the Bestlite by Robert Dudley Best has been in continuous production since it was designed in the 1930s. The wall-mounted version is seen here as a bedside lamp, but desk and floor-standing versions are still made by Best and Lloyd.**
bottom right **A basic but efficient design, this aluminium light has an extendable arm and an adjustable head to focus on the work in hand.**

freestanding lamps

Table lamps and floor lamps create an inviting atmosphere by lowering the visual focus to a more intimate level and drawing groups of furniture together in their circle of light.

Moveable lamps are usually an addition to a lighting scheme rather than its main feature, and set against a background of ambient or general light they create an expressive balance of light and shade that is somewhat lacking in rooms lit entirely from above.

Table lamps are the most widely used freestanding fittings and come in all shapes, sizes and styles. The material the shade is made from has most bearing on the type and colour of light it provides. Translucent materials like textiles and parchment give a diffuse light while shades made from opaque materials such as metal direct light up and down. Closely related to the table lamp is the floor lamp. This umbrella term encompasses everything from a traditional standard lamp down to low-level lights that are really oversized table lamps providing functional or decorative light.

above far left and centre **The Akari light sculptures created by Japanese artist Isamu Noguchi and produced throughout the second half of the 20th century have become icons of 1950s design. Like all Noguchi lights, the UFI-C** (left) **and the 22N** (centre) **lamps are Modernist in form but made in the traditional Japanese style from mulberry-bark paper with bamboo ribbing on a metal frame. These lamps are available from the Isamu Noguchi Garden Museum Store.** above near left **Designed like a contemporary candlestick, the slender Whizz table lamp, by Markus Hürsch for Lumess, has a cylindrical opaque white 'candle' that glows with inner light.** below far left **An unusual light like this rock-shaped floor lamp is more an illuminated object than a light source. By** highlighting its own slightly granular surface it draws attention to the contrasting textures of the glass, wicker, limestone and timber surrounding it. A similar floor lamp is the Glo-ball by Jasper Morrison for Flos. below centre **A period light fitting can be the signature of a historically inspired room scheme or, if the design is sufficiently distinctive, stand alone as a decorative object in a room that does not share its stylistic origins. This antique desk lamp spotlights the silver box standing next to it, amplifying the Art Deco style of both objects.** below near left **With the light switched on, the Rabane shade from The Conran Shop is transformed from wholesome, natural wickerwork to a glowing mesh weaving shadows across the wall.**

above near right **The natural colour and grain of wood veneer change dramatically when it is backlit. This woven veneer shade by Peter Wylly is no longer available, but similar contemporary, non-woven wood designs can be found.**

above centre **An uplighter-cum-wallwasher with an industrial aesthetic, this unconventional lamp constructed from recycled materials was designed and made by François Muracciole. More sculptural than decorative, it demands to stand alone where it can be appreciated for its appearance and its lighting effect.**

far right, above and below **This wooden floor-standing lamp was designed by Frank Lloyd Wright for his Arizona home, Taliesin West. Its linear design echoes the vertical rails in the neighbouring chair, also designed by Wright. The lamp incorporates a shelf positioned midway below the light to hold a small vase of flowers.**

below near right **More Art Nouveau than Arts and Crafts, this sinuous lily-pad lamp with glass trumpet shades is seen here in the bedroom of a house designed by American Arts and Crafts architects Greene & Greene, where it lends a touch of frivolity. Lamps like this can be found in specialist antique shops and some excellent reproductions are available, such as that from 4 Desk Table Lamps & Shades and Christopher Wray.**

below centre left **There is something solidly workmanlike in this table lamp with its five-sided thick wooden base and wide-leaded glass shade. A reproduction of an Arts and Crafts original, it is not seen in its full glory until the lamp is switched on and the colours of the stained glass glow with a jewel-like brilliance.**

below centre **Designed in the 1960s and currently undergoing a revival, the lava lamp is colourful and fascinating to watch. The clear lamp contains coloured water and wax in a contrasting colour which, when melted by the heat of the bulb, rises through the water. This Telstar model is now discontinued but Mathmos make five similar lamps.**

below centre right **Elegant and contemporary, with a slightly animated posture, the Kow Tow table lamp by Charlotte Packe has a cream parchment shade and a flexible stem made from discs of anodized, spun aluminium.**

controls

Flexible controls are key to the success of a lighting scheme and should be considered at an early stage in its design. Where they go, what they do and how they look all have a dramatic effect on the room.

Switches control lighting by turning fittings on and off, individually or in groups, or by dimming them. Some sophisticated controls can memorize pre-programmed lighting 'scenes', allowing you literally to turn on the atmosphere at the flick of a switch. Others can be time- or remote-controlled for convenience.

There is a style of light switch to suit every room, with brass or Bakelite dome switches for period homes and for classic or contemporary interiors, square or rectangular switchplates in black, white or coloured plastic, clear Perspex, wood and virtually any metallic finish you choose. The working part of the control can be a dolly or rocker switch to turn the light on and off or a knob to operate a dimmer.

opposite and above left **Electrical wiring is usually chased into plasterwork to do its job unseen, but here it is carried over the surface of the wall through a metal conduit to supply a stainless-steel surface-mounted switch. The aesthetic success of surface wiring depends on meticulous installation with straight conduits and neat joins.**

top left **It is unusual to find a bank of four dimmer switches on a single plate but they can be made to order by specialist electrical suppliers.**

top centre **The Meljac push-button momentary dimmer from SKK is a minimal and intelligent control. You flick the button to turn the lights on or off, or press and hold to lower the light to the required level. The switch will store the previous dimmer setting in its memory.**

top right **Virtually invisible with only the control knobs apparent, a clear switchplate gives a sophisticated finish to a room. Similar clear Perspex switchplates are available from Forbes & Lomax.**

above centre **When there are a number of lights in the same room, controls can be arranged in rows on a single switchplate or, as here, arranged singly and in pairs on separate plates. Old-fashioned dolly switches are suitable for a traditionally furnished room and look best on a plain, flat plate.**

above right **Designer Patti Seidman believes that you turn lights on and off more often than you adjust the level of light and finds that the Lutron Diva switch, which has a large on-off rocker switch and a separate lever to dim the light, conforms to those priorities.**

KITCHENS

AS THE BARRIERS BETWEEN LIVING ROOMS AND KITCHENS COME DOWN, THE PLACE WHERE

WE COOK BECOMES OPEN TO SCRUTINY – ALL THE MORE REASON TO REASSESS THE WAY

IT LOOKS AND WORKS. CABINETS AND SURFACES COME IN EVERY KIND OF WOOD, STONE,

LAMINATE AND PAINTED FINISH OR IN SUPER-CHIC MATERIALS LIKE GLASS AND METAL.

AND TAPS, SINKS AND APPLIANCES ARE MORE STYLISH AND EFFICIENT THAN EVER.

kitchen units

A new openness in living space has brought changes into the kitchen. No longer hidden behind closed doors, it is a place to be shared with family and friends – and it must look good.

Over the last few decades, the kitchen has undergone a remarkable shift in status. From a utilitarian space for the preparation of food, it has become an integral part of the home, where cooking, eating and entertaining take place side by side. Accordingly, it is furnished as thoughtfully, and expensively, as the living room. The idea of a kitchen in which you would eat out of choice rather than necessity emerged in the 1970s, when a pine farmhouse kitchen with a scrubbed table was the ideal. The image was one of warmth and hospitality, the hub of family life. Now, instead of living in the kitchen, open-plan layouts have changed the emphasis so it is more a case of cooking in the living room – a setup made all the more possible by improvements in air extraction and virtually silent appliances.

Kitchen units, too, have moved on, and cupboards faced with metal, glass and even stone are as much an option as polished or painted wood and laminates. Even the familiar finishes are developing with changing trends, as exotic timber veneers and high-gloss laminates give a sharper, urban look.

left **Appearing to defy the laws of gravity, this cooking alcove suspended from the ceiling allows an uninterrupted sweep of glossy black floor to give a feeling of continuity and space. The alcove was custom-made, though some IKEA kitchen carcasses were adapted and used in its construction.**

opposite, above left **Sharp contrast conveys urban sophistication in this slick yellow and black kitchen with Formica-laminated cabinets and slate worktops.**

opposite, above right **This traditionally inspired blue and cream kitchen has an island unit at its centre to make practical use of a large floor area.**

opposite, centre left **Designed to appear as a heavy stone block hovering above the floor, this unit is cantilevered from the wall with additional support from a ceiling-mounted pillar which also carries the power supply. The unit is faced with beige pietro laro limestone and fitted with spray-lacquered doors.**

opposite, centre **Horizontal lines dominate this kitchen where the contrasting stripes of the tall cabinet are echoed in the timber banding of the wall units.**

opposite, centre right **Made from distinctively grained crown-cut oak, this horizontal unit provides efficient storage and is a good-looking piece of furniture.**

opposite, below left **Built from IKEA units fitted with custom-made MDF doors, the angles and curves of these cupboards were developed by computer and are linked by their strong colours.**

opposite, below centre **In order to screen and contain the clutter of cooking, this rank of cabinets is enclosed on three sides by taller panels, with electrical sockets built into the upstand.**

opposite, below right **Cubic cupboards arranged like building blocks make full use of an impressive wall height.**

Architect-designed kitchens have always had the edge on those from standard ranges, but the gap between the two is gradually narrowing as kitchen manufacturers are willing to build bespoke cabinets or at least customize existing designs to meet individual demands. This break from strictly modular design has opened the way for more interesting and inventive use of space.

Conventional fitted kitchens take the form of deep floor-standing base units with smaller wall-mounted cupboards above, but in the interests of creating a more open, spacious effect, wall units are now used more sparingly. Where they are used, ease of access has been addressed with tambour shutters and up-and-over doors offering space-saving alternatives to side-hinged doors that swing out at head height. If wall cupboards are lost, storage must be found elsewhere, and one of the most efficient alternatives is to build a bank of floor-to-ceiling cupboards fitted with shelves, drawers and racks and incorporating the fridge and freezer. In most kitchens, a wall of cupboards like this would supply enough storage to allow worktops – often seconded as overflow shelf space – to be left clear.

New ideas for base units also contribute to a more spacious look, with some designers exploring the possibilities of 'floating' units. These are cabinets supported on strong, cantilevered brackets from an adjoining wall or suspended from joists in the ceiling. The result is an unbroken sweep of floor and an impression of space and continuity. Where it is not possible to physically lift the units off the floor, a similar effect can be achieved by recessing the kickboard at the foot of the unit and fitting lights invisibly into the space.

opposite, left **This kitchen was reinvented using some carcasses salvaged from the existing cupboards. The new MDF doors were professionally spray-painted for a perfect finish, in colours inspired by an exhibition catalogue for London's Design Museum. Laminate worktops and splashbacks and polished aluminium handles enhance the retro style.**

opposite, above right **Two solutions to the problem of small-scale storage: a rack of glass jars holds seasonings where they are easy to identify, and neat square drawers with finger-hole pulls are just the right size for dry ingredients, small utensils, string, scissors and other vital but hard-to-place items.**

opposite, centre right **Shimmering aluminium-framed sandblasted-glass cabinets, steel appliances and white marble worktops create a cool translucent effect. Wide drawers and concealed storage ensure that nothing need be left on the surfaces to detract from the pale perfection of the materials.**

opposite, below right **Pan scrubs, brushes and cloths are an inescapable part of the kitchen-sink landscape, but this tilt-out sponge tray by Feeny, available in stainless steel or plastic, fits into the fascia in front of the sink to hide them from view.**

this page, top left **A modern interpretation of a pantry, this cabinet opens to give a clear view of its entire contents. Storage is divided between open shelves and metal racking on the insides of the doors; both are adjustable too, so can be moved to suit changing storage demands. The interior of the pantry is made from pale birch plywood which reflects light into the shelf cavities.**

this page, above left **Concentrating storage in a wall of floor-to-ceiling cupboards makes economical use of space and results in a 'hidden kitchen' where all food and utensils are concealed, leaving worktops clear. Here, storage is arranged in three tiers. The middle cabinets, housing small appliances such as a coffee-maker and toaster, have flip-down doors that can be used as surfaces when using those items.**

this page, above right **A combination of sleek materials adds glamour to this conventional galley kitchen. The base cabinets are veneered with dark-stained Italian poplar in contrast to the light maple and sandblasted glass wall units. The work surface and square sink are made from the same silky black honed granite. The sink is set on an open shelf with half-height cupboards beneath.**

surfaces

Your kitchen worktop and splashback must be up to the job: choose high-performance materials that offer good looks, too.

The ideal work surface is durable, hygienic, quiet, stain resistant and heatproof; but as no one material can claim ownership to all of these qualities, a compromise must be reached, and appearance is invariably the deciding factor. The choice lies between natural materials like wood and stone, which tend to complement each other, or synthetics such as laminates and resins, which, depending on their style and quality, can be successfully combined with units made of natural or manmade materials.

opposite, above **This brilliant blue-veined worktop and splashback are made from a Brazilian granite, azul macauba, which contains precious lapis lazuli.**

opposite, centre left **Damage from sharp knives and hot pans can be removed from natural wood surfaces by rubbing them down with abrasive paper. Oil newly sanded surfaces to seal and protect them.**

opposite, centre **This chef's trolley is topped with a functional beech-wood chopping board and slides neatly away into a cupboard when not in use.**

opposite, centre right **This breakfast bar is built from custom-made laminated board in a barcode stripe designed by Filer & Cox.**

opposite, below left **An unusual large-scale terrazzo, this crazy patchwork of marble fragments is ground smooth to produce a practical but eccentric surface.**

opposite, below centre **Using the same batique blue limestone for the floor and work surfaces gives a sense of space and consistency. The soft grey-blue of the stone has an affinity with the light elm cabinets.**

opposite, below right **This wavy-edged worktop is formed from thick plywood cut to shape, sanded and sealed so the layers of laminated wood show as striped edging.**

above right **The concrete worktop and side panel, cast on site by a local contractor, form a continuous hard shell around the stained and limed white ash veneer cabinets.**

right **Marble is smooth, cool and famously ideal for pastry making. It is also vulnerable to staining if not properly sealed and cared for. This 4-cm-thick Carrara marble has a silky honed finish – less hard- and new-looking than polished marble. Large slabs mean joints are kept to a minimum.**

this page, above left and top right **Sleek and cool, glass is a sophisticated and surprisingly practical choice of worktop for a modern kitchen. This kitchen, by VX Design, is part of an open-plan living area and uses translucent materials for most of its hard surfaces. The island is wrapped in toughened etched glass, as is the narrow arching bar.**

this page, above right **This shelf in a cook's kitchen is often filled to overflowing but a low rail fitted around the edge prevents bottles slipping off the smooth surface.**

opposite, above left **Stainless steel for the worktop and high splashback offers a neutral yet lively balance for the vivid pink units in this family kitchen. Most stainless-steel worktops are made to measure and can be supplied with integral sinks in**
a variety of configurations. The splashback, too, has been customized to incorporate a narrow shelf along its entire length to hold frequently used crockery, glass and ingredients.

opposite, above right **Instead of imposing its own style, a stainless-steel worktop takes on the character of its surroundings. The cabinets in this dazzling white kitchen are made from a high-gloss laminate in the Op-art Morphscape pattern designed by its owner, Karim Rasheed. The stainless-steel worktop and splashback reflect the predominantly white laminate and appear light, bright and silvery.**

opposite, centre left **The great advantage of stainless steel is that it can be formed into many shapes, so different components can be made from the same material to give complete continuity. Straight rails**
fixed along the front of the work surface are handy for hanging teatowels or utensils while you work.

opposite, below left **Brushed steel is the most forgiving metal surface, its soft sheen tactfully camouflaging fingermarks. Designed and made by John Barman Inc., this kitchen shows off the quality of the metal and its industrial aesthetic by keeping detail to a minimum with perfectly flat door and drawer fronts punctuated by tiny functional knobs.**

opposite, below right **The epitome of a professional-style kitchen, stainless steel is used over all the main surfaces here, including the island worktop. Tough, hygienic and heatproof, it can stand up to the rigours of a hard-working kitchen. The only drawback is that it can be noisy to work on, but this can be overcome with proper insulation.**

plumbing

Good plumbing is an essential aspect of kitchen design and one that has not been neglected by architects and designers, who offer taps and sinks that are both striking in appearance and supremely efficient.

No kitchen can function without a ready, reliable and easily controlled water supply and a sink in which to rinse food, wash hands and do the dishes. Plumbing may have a less than glamorous image, but it is an area of interest for designers, intrigued by the engineering and aesthetic challenge. Distinguished designers like Arne Jacobsen and Philippe Starck have designed taps that achieved iconic status, but there are many more, conceived by unsung designers, that fulfil their purpose with style and efficiency.

Kitchen taps are made to a number of basic patterns, the oldest being the bibcock – a deck- or wall-mounted tap with a spout and crosshead handle. Mixer taps deliver hot and cold water from the same spout but have separate handwheels or levers to control the supply. They can be deck or wall mounted, traditional or modern in style, and are fitted via two or three holes drilled in the surface. Monobloc

top row, far left **Designed to appear smaller than it really is, this unusual portrait-shaped stainless-steel sink is recessed into the wall as well as the worktop. The wall-mounted Vola mixer tap with swivel spout was designed by Arne Jacobsen.**

top row, centre left **Bib taps on upstands match the traditional style of a Belfast sink and are set high enough to avoid catching dishes when they are lifted in and out of the sink.**

top row, centre right **A double-bowl sink is useful for food preparation but provision must be made for draining. Many manufacturers supply drainer baskets or trays to fit their sinks as separate accessories. A swivel-spout mixer tap like this elegantly arched monobloc fitting is essential for a double-bowl sink. A similar tap is the Petita by Grohe.**

top row, near left **In a kitchen where superfluous detail is kept to a minimum and low-sheen surfaces prevail, the satin-steel Arwa-Twin, with a pull-out spout, by Gemini Bath and Kitchen Products fills the stainless-steel double sink mounted under a thick marble surface.**

middle row, far left **A wall-mounted hospital mixer tap transplants smoothly into a small kitchen where its slender shape and pivoting spout fit the restricted space. Similar hospital- and laboratory-style taps are available from T & S Brass.**

middle row, centre left **An inventive plumber has created this tap from pipes and valves usually hidden from view. Check local and national building and water regulations before constructing a similar tap.**

middle row, centre right **As neat and compact as the circular sink it fills, this monobloc tap has a single lever that controls both temperature and flow. The Allegra range by Hansgrohe has similar designs with and without a pull-out spray.**

middle row, near left **A nostalgic style for a country kitchen, this mixer tap, similar to the Colonial by Bristan and the Victorian models by Harrington Brass and Gemini, has a brushed finish for a time-worn effect.**

bottom row, far left **Taps with a pull-out brush do not comply with regulations in some countries, but the alternative pull-out spray is more widely accepted. The Europlus by Grohe is similar in appearance to the one shown here but has a spray for rinsing vegetables and sluicing plates.**

bottom row, centre left **White ceramic levers give an arched monobloc tap a period look.**

bottom row, centre right **A compact swan-neck monobloc tap similar to the Ostende by Herbeau supplies a small hammered metal sink used for preparing vegetables.**

bottom row, near left **Plumbing goes back to basics in this rustic kitchen with a Belfast sink mounted on a countertop and supplied by garden taps on the wall above.**

fittings are the newest type and are consequently modern in design. Deck mounted through a single hole in the sink or work surface, they consist of a spout with separate handles to control the hot and cold flow or a single lever handle that controls temperature and flow at once. The latest developments in tap design are mixer fittings with a third handle that allows purified drinking water as well as hot and cold water to flow from the same spout, and monobloc taps which incorporate a pull-out hose and rinsing spray. Finishes are many and varied, ranging from shiny, satin and antique metals to coloured plain and speckled effects.

The kitchen sink, once a symbol of drudgery, has shaken off its depressing associations and is now a visually important feature of

the kitchen. Sinks may be made from ceramic, stainless steel, brass, synthetic or real stone, and even wood, and are set into, under or between work surfaces. Various configurations are available, of which a single sink and drainer unit is the most basic, and an angled sink to fit the corner of a kitchen probably the most unusual. Double sinks are a popular choice, and many can be fitted with a waste-disposal unit to deal with wet waste from food preparation. Sinks must incorporate some provision for draining in the form of an attached draining board, grooves cut into the adjoining waterproof work surface or a basket that fits into one of the sinks. The only exception to this is where an additional sink is inset into an island unit for the purpose of straining food from saucepans.

opposite, top left **This traditional bridge mixer tap with an upwardly angled 'cranked' spout was chosen in preference to the arching swan-neck type for its compact shape. Made by Samuel Heath, the shiny chrome finish adds a sparkle to the predominantly white scheme.**

opposite, above left **A modified shower mixer makes an interesting kitchen tap with a flexible spout, but may not comply with regulations governing water fittings in all areas. A similar effect can be achieved with a purpose-made tap designed for**
commercial kitchens, such as the Pro-chef by Brass & Traditional Sinks.

opposite, right **A classic minimalist design by architect and designer Dieter Sieger, the Tara Classic mixer tap and soap dispenser produced by Dornbracht make a fitting centrepiece for this practical stainless-steel sink area. Note the downlighters fitted flush into the underside of the wall cabinets to provide bright illumination for the sink and work surface.**

this page, main picture **In this sleek, rather masculine kitchen, the overall effect is one of understated luxury.**
The work surface with its integral sink is made from black honed granite, which has a gleaming satin surface far removed from the hard gloss of polished stone. The splashback is a continuous stainless-steel surface, brushed to a low sheen. The tap, a design icon, is the Vola KV1 kitchen mixer by Arne Jacobsen.

top right **All-metal mixer taps with lever handles have a minimalist, almost clinical appearance, but the clean and functional design that makes them so suitable for use in hospitals and laboratories is equally**
appropriate in the kitchen. This tap is made in the United States by T & S Brass, but similar designs can be found in ranges made for hospitals by manufacturers such as Barber Wilsons.

above right **Another architects' favourite, little known on the commercial scene, this tap with star-shaped handles – made in Denmark by Toni Armatur – is a beautifully pared-down design, engineered to last. Teamed with an integral stainless-steel sink and worktop, it contributes towards the air of professional efficiency in this kitchen.**

appliances

Not so long ago kitchen appliances were hidden away, only evident when they shuddered into action. Now, technology has reordered priorities and, like Victorian children, they are seen but rarely heard.

Appliances are the essential working parts of a kitchen and exert a strong influence on its style. Freestanding models are weighty and solid, with a distinctive character. In recent years, cookers and fridges have increased in size, with industrial models entering the domestic environment and farmhouse stoves moving to the city. Built-in appliances are sleek, streamlined and make economical use of space in urban kitchens, where the coffee-maker is now as likely to be built in as the oven or dishwasher. Designed for looks as well as performance, these machines are no longer hidden behind cupboard doors and décor panels but have become fashion items, carrying the household equivalent of designer labels. In tandem with aesthetic developments, technology has improved domestic machines with efficient and quiet running, while energy labelling allows consumers to choose those that make least impact on the environment and their pockets.

opposite, above **A monolithic double-door refrigerator like this one from the professional Monogram range by General Electric could dominate a kitchen, but its stainless-steel finish offers some camouflage amidst the other metallic surfaces. Inside, the space is divided into temperature zones to provide prime storage conditions for different foods.**
opposite, below left **A stainless-steel dishwasher from the Gallery range by Frigidaire is quiet-running and fits the industrial aesthetic of this all-metal**

kitchen. Part of its attraction is its simple design with discreet controls and an easy-to-grip handle.
opposite, below centre **This Monogram microwave by General Electric is actually a countertop model, but it has been slotted in to purpose-made housing at eye level to give a fully fitted look and leave the work surfaces clear.**
opposite, below right **Framed in an alcove, this bright blue fridge-freezer by Boffi adds a lively splash of colour to a neutral kitchen.**

above left and centre **An intelligent design, the DishDrawer dishwasher by Fisher & Paykel has two independently operated pull-out washing units. One can be used alone when there are only a few dishes to wash or they can be used together on different settings to wash delicate crystal and heavily soiled saucepans.**
top right **In a small kitchen where open shelves have been fitted instead of wall cabinets to provide high-level storage, the KitchenAid microwave oven is placed in a wall-mounted box**

shelf, slightly deeper than the rest, with just enough space left over to slip in a few favourite cookery books.
above right **This fridge-freezer stands at one end of a rank of fitted units and, although it is freestanding, it has clearly been planned into the layout at an early stage. Base and wall cabinets are positioned to leave a space into which it fits perfectly, and its stainless-steel finish implies a relationship with the work surface and other appliances, though they are not all from the same manufacturer.**

this page, above **A built-under oven with a hob fitted above it looks like a single cooking unit but is more streamlined than a freestanding cooker and saves space in a small kitchen. Usually the hob and oven are selected from the same collection, but appliances from different manufacturers can be teamed up to give the combination of features required. Here, an oven from the Gallery range by Frigidaire is installed under an Amana gas hob.**

this page, below left **This curved concrete worktop was cast on site with plywood moulds to form indentations into which the hob units were later fitted. Modular hobs like these by Smeg allow a more flexible kitchen layout, especially when the work surface is not a conventional shape.**

this page, below right **Specially designed for healthy eaters, the extra-wide hob on the Viking 36-inch (91-cm) range cooker incorporates a griddle-simmer plate.**

opposite, above left and above centre **The migration of the professional cooker into the domestic kitchen is complete, and heavy-duty range cookers like this Viking freestanding model have become a familiar feature. Built for efficiency, every detail is designed to make cooking safer and easier. The pan supports, for example, are made from strong cast iron configured to support small pans without tipping and to allow large, heavy pans to slide over them without lifting.**

opposite, above right **Hob covers leave the kitchen looking neat when not in use. This Gaggenau hob has a divided shot-blasted aluminium lid that folds down over two or four burners.**

opposite, centre left **A powerful cooker hood is essential when the kitchen forms part of an open-plan living area, and this Miele Combiset hood is available as an extractor, venting to the outside, or as a filter, cleaning and re-circulating the air.**

opposite, below left **For convenience, store frequently used utensils around the hob. Here, a hanging rail extends across the splashback, and the Bosch cooker hood has been fitted with an optional chrome wire shelf strong enough to hold saucepans.**

opposite, below right **The Viking range cooker comes in four sizes, from 30–60 inches (75–150 cm) wide. It was designed for professional kitchens but has a standard depth measurement that allows it to slot between fitted units.**

opposite, above left **The chimneybreast and alcove were specially built to accommodate this reconditioned 1940s Aga, with a 'supporting' beam from a reclamation yard for authenticity. Reproduction Agas in 1930s styles are now available for those who want a period look without tracking down an original.**

opposite, above centre **Modern Agas, while still distinctively traditional in style, offer a choice of fuels and come in a range of classic and fashionable colours, including the original cream.**

opposite, above right **A combination microwave oven is stacked above a single oven, both from Bosch, creating a mid-height cooking unit at the end of a run of units.**

this page, above left **A pair of ceramic hob modules by General Electric, virtually flush with the worktop, sit neatly side by side above a matching wide built-under oven.**

this page, above centre **An inset single burner is a useful addition to the main hob in a large kitchen; in addition many manufacturers produce independent built-in wok burners.**

this page, above right **A refined version of the industrial range cooker, this has twin ovens, a wide hob and integral splashback and hood. Similar models are made by Smeg and Britannia.**

below far left **Independent hob modules like this Domino unit by Smeg allow you to place a cook-top where you need it.**

below centre and near left centre **In this sleek kitchen, cooking appliances are centralized in a single stack, with a built-in coffee-maker perched at eye level above the Miele double oven. A tall, pull-out larder unit separates the ovens from the nearby Sub-Zero fridge.**

below near left **An island unit composed of an oval stainless-steel countertop with a Smeg hob supported on a cylindrical wooden cupboard makes a contemporary statement.**

155

BATHROOMS

WHEN A TUB CAN COST AS MUCH AS A FAMILY CAR, YOU KNOW THE BATHROOM HAS BECOME A FASHION ITEM. MATERIAL IS THE WATCHWORD AS BATHS ARE NOW MADE IN ANYTHING FROM LOW-COST ACRYLICS TO INDUSTRIAL STAINLESS STEEL AND LUXURY LIMESTONE. BASINS ARE FASHIONED FROM GLASS, MARBLE AND WOOD AS WELL AS COOL, GLOSSY CERAMICS, AND WALLS AND FLOORS ARE SURFACED IN FINISHES AS DIVERSE AS CONCRETE, WOOD AND MOSAIC.

opposite, above left **This bathroom has a modern elegance that combines the transparency of glass and the substance of teak. The bath, designed by architects Azman Owens, has glass sides and timber ends. The basin, undermounted beneath a glass countertop, has a fascia of teak panels concealing drawers.**

opposite, above right **At the centre of this traditional bathroom stands a Jazz oval steel bath from C.P. Hart. The surround was made to order from laminated timber with a machined wood base, all painted with a faux-stone effect and edged with a limestone rim.**

opposite, centre left **This sleek and gleaming stainless-steel surround was specially made to fit an enamelled cast-iron bath by Düker, but a similar oval bath and surround can be found in the Philosophy collection by Sottini.**

opposite, below left **Most timbers are damaged or discoloured by water, but teak shrugs off splashes. Here, its rich colour brings warmth and a masculine edge to a traditional bathroom.**

opposite, below right **A modern take on the traditional roll-top bath, this enamelled cast-iron Betty bath by Alternative Plans has a flattened rim and is cradled on specially made solid-oak rests instead of ball-and-claw feet.**

above right **This stainless-steel bath, designed by architects Tsao and McKown, was custom-made with an undulating base to allow bathing in a comfortable position. Stainless-steel fabricators can be commissioned to produce baths to order.**

far right above **The deep green mosaic of the sunken bath contrasts with the surrounding floor to give an illusion of depth.**

far right below **Opaque corrugated glass-reinforced plastic, of the kind usually seen on the roofs of greenhouses, makes a practical and inexpensive bath surround.**

fittings

Bathroom design is increasingly flexible and is now more likely to be tailored to match the owner's lifestyle than any preconceived format. Yet the essential fittings are still a bath, handbasin and lavatory, with a separate shower enclosure and bidet as optional but desirable extras.

In most bathrooms, the bathtub is the dominating feature. Tubs don't have to be bought as part of a suite, though some manufacturers offer a small range of shapes to complement their ceramic fittings. Baths are most commonly made from acrylic, enamelled steel or porcelain-enamelled cast iron, but new materials such as acrylic resin – a warm-to-the-touch non-chip substitute for cast iron – are becoming more popular. Apart from standard materials, baths in stainless steel, limestone or hardwood are an option, but these are usually made to order and therefore more expensive.

Bath shapes vary widely and as well as the standard rectangular tub which comes in sizes to fit most bathrooms there are tapered baths for small spaces, corner baths for awkward spaces and freestanding baths in traditional and modern styles. Antique roll-top baths made from cast iron with ball-and-claw feet can be bought in original condition from architectural salvage yards or restored from dealers specializing in antique bathroom fittings. Alternatively, reproduction roll-top baths made from cast iron or acrylic resin are available from most bathroom suppliers. Most modern freestanding baths are made from acrylic resin and stand alone or enclosed within a purpose-built cabinet.

A shower is a high priority for most for new bathrooms. Where space is limited, it can be mounted over the bath, but a separate enclosure or area is always the ideal. Those who prefer showering to bathing may opt for a large shower area instead of a bath (but estate agents maintain that properties with at least one bathtub are easier to sell than those with none). A shower can be bought as a self-contained cabinet or built on site using the existing walls, new stud-partition walls, glass-brick walls or safety-glass shower panels, with a sliding, folding, hinged or pivoting glass door. The enclosure must be lined with tiles or some other waterproof surface and sealed to prevent seepage. A shower tray, generally made from glazed ceramic, enamelled steel or acrylic, can form the floor. Alternatively, in a

above left **The custom-made neon green Perspex shower screen and vanity shelf add a lively, reflective dimension in a small shower room.**

centre left **The glowing golden interior of this circular shower enclosure was constructed on site by gluing together three layers of 6 mm birch plywood. Veneer was applied to conceal the horizontal joint and the whole surface was sealed against moisture with several coats of marine varnish.**

below left **The walls in this wet room were coated with natural sand and cement render and made waterproof with a clear sealant. On the floor, the honed limestone slabs are spaced to allow water to drain through to an outlet beneath.**

below centre **Mosaic tiles in assorted shades of blue bring colour into this shower room, and a wall of textured glass bricks allows daylight in.**

below right **This shower enclosure was designed to let natural light spill through. The unit comprises a curve of sandblasted glass custom-made to fit**

around a circular stainless-steel base – both were made to order by local contractors.

opposite, above **The airy character of this bathroom has been preserved by zoning the space with custom-made transparent glass panels.**

opposite, below left **A circular enclosure formed from frosted glass makes a roomy shower cabinet, top-lit for brilliant illumination. A shower tower, similar to the Taron by Grohe, supplies water through a fixed showerhead and hand spray.**

opposite, below centre **The classical style of this bathroom required unobtrusive fittings, and the frameless shower door, similar to those in the Majestic range, allows the eye to pass through to the honey-coloured stone-clad interior.**

opposite, below right **In this wet room, oblong glass bricks shield the shower area. The floor is tiled with limestone and the walls are finished in hardwall plaster. The porous surfaces were all treated with a stone-waterproofing sealant by Lithofin.**

bathroom designed as a wet room with walls and floor fully waterproofed, the shower needs no enclosure and the water escapes through a central drain in the floor. The shower itself may be fed from the domestic hot and cold water supply or, where an electric shower is fitted, from the mains water supply. Showers perform well only if there is sufficient water pressure, but where the pressure is too low a pump can usually be installed to boost the flow.

To meet the demand for different shapes, sizes and styles, washbasins come in a variety of materials, with glazed ceramic basins being the traditional choice. These are available in a range of colours and are tough, easy to clean and available to buy off the shelf. With a choice of pedestal, wall-mounted, inset and under-mounted countertop basins, they are often designed as part of a suite of matching fittings, taking some of the decision-making out of the process of bathroom design. However, interesting stand-alone models are available if you want the basin to be the focus of the room. Beautiful and surprisingly resilient, glass basins can also be bought ready-made, but the choice is limited to small or medium round bowls in a range of colours and

opposite, above left **A compact design, ideal for a small cloakroom, this tubby wall-mounted basin by Agape goes by the descriptive name of Cheese.**

opposite, above centre **This satinized-glass basin is part of an all-in-one wall-mounted unit incorporating a mixer tap, plumbing and bracket and known as the Pollux 1. The combination of translucent and reflective materials gives it a lack of solidity that makes it a good choice for a small bathroom.**

opposite, above right **Concrete is favoured for its industrial chic and can be used to custom-make hardwearing surfaces of all kinds. This basin, designed and cast by Philip Wish, has a wide, shallow bowl and deep ledges at the sides.**

opposite, below left **Designed to relieve the morning rush hour when everyone is getting ready at the same time, this long glass design is more streamlined than the usual twin basins. Custom made by Jeff Bell, it is shallow and gently angled to ensure efficient emptying.**

opposite, centre right **Masculine in character, this straight-sided rectangular basin made from 30-mm-thick grey limestone is built wide enough for more enthusiastic washing than a smaller hand-rinse basin would allow. The mixer spout and pop-up waste control are placed to one side and the handles are fitted to the front of the countertop.**

opposite, below right **In a small bathroom where there is little scope for adventurous decoration, fittings with an unusual design feature make the space more interesting. The wall-mounted Scola basin by Duravit, for example, has a circular bowl set into a rectangular surround.**

above **The shape of this square basin from Colourwash is accentuated by its setting on a custom-made brushed stainless-steel base. Inside, the sharp angles give way to smooth curves for easier cleaning.**

right **Stainless-steel fittings give the bathroom a functional look, but this bespoke basin's elegant shape eliminates any hint of institutional severity.**

above **A high-level cast-iron cistern is usually an original fitting in a period bathroom, but makers of traditional bathroom fittings, such as B.C. Sanitan, supply ceramic ones for a similar look.**
right **In this circular frosted-glass cloakroom pod, the ultra-modern basin and lavatory stand in the centre of the space with drainage ducted through the floor. Overhead spotlights combine with polished steel and glass to gleaming effect.**
opposite, above left **In small bathrooms, a toilet with a flush valve instead of a cistern can help save space. Widespread in the United States, flush valves are less common in Britain, where the mains water pressure is not always sufficiently high.**
opposite, centre left **In a sophisticated setting, a stainless-steel lavatory has a stylish industrial aesthetic. This one is wall mounted on a sturdy bracket with a concealed cistern. Similar stainless-steel models are made by Santric.**
opposite, above right **A narrow rectangular cistern and conical bowl combine in the uncompromisingly contemporary Starck close-coupled lavatory by Duravit.**
opposite, below left **A floor-standing bidet with a traditional waisted shape, the London bidet is shown here with a rounded crosshead Leonardo mixer from C.P. Hart.**
opposite, below centre **The wall-hung model of the Starck lavatory, with a concealed cistern, is the ultimate minimalist design.**
opposite, below right **For a luxury look with a modern edge, choose fittings with smoothly rounded edges but no extraneous decoration. The Allora by Jacuzzi is similar in shape to this wall-mounted lavatory.**

finishes. This restriction only applies to ready-made basins; bespoke glass bowls can be produced in much larger sizes and non-standard shapes and designs. At the more exclusive end of the market are basins made from unconventional materials such as wood, stone, marble, plywood and, less expensively, stainless steel.

Lavatories come in styles to suit every taste, but one practical way in which they can differ is in the type of cistern they have. Most common is the close-coupled cistern that sits at the back of the bowl giving the appearance of an all-in-one unit. Low-level cisterns are wall-mounted with a flush pipe connecting the cistern to the bowl, and traditional high-level cisterns are wall-mounted on decorative brackets with a long pipe to the bowl and a pull chain to operate the flush. Concealed cisterns, usually used with back-to-wall and wall-mounted lavatories, are fitted behind a false wall or panel with only the flush handle or button visible.

Bidets are a convenient way to deal with personal hygiene and are usually situated alongside the lavatory. They are filled by a monobloc mixer with an directional nozzle to angle the water flow, and, like lavatories, can be floor standing or wall mounted.

taps & controls

Adjusting water temperature is a matter of safety as well as convenience, so controls must be easy to operate by everyone, including children and the elderly. Clear labelling is vital, particularly in showers, where a handle turned the wrong way can result in a rush of scalding water.

Bathroom taps come in three main formats: three-hole mixers where the handles and spout are separate; mixers that are single units incorporating spout and handles or a single lever; and traditional pillar taps with separate outlets for hot and cold. Basin mixers often incorporate a pop-up waste control, while bath mixers may also feed a shower, with a handle to divert water from one function to the other. Shower controls can be thermostatic or mechanical: thermostatic controls deliver water at a preset temperature, while mechanical showers are adjusted manually to achieve the right temperature.

top row, far left **Overhead showers give a thorough drenching, and in a large enclosure, two sprays ensure even coverage. However, two showers deliver twice the volume of water, so a large waste will be needed for efficient drainage. A similar shower for overhead fixing is the Aktiva by Hansgrohe.**

top row, centre left **These four-square chunky traditional-looking controls are mixers for the bath and shower. The chrome crosshead handles are the Regent design by Barber Wilsons.**

top row, centre right **A dual-control thermostatic shower mixer has one handle to control the water flow and another to adjust the temperature. This fitting by Hansgrohe is now available as a design that has both handles on one plate.**

top row, near left **Designed to remain free of limescale, this showerhead has tiny projections that keep the jets clear. A similar showerhead is the Fez by Agape.**

middle row, far left **White enamelled taps were popular in the 1970s and 1980s, and look good in an all-white bathroom. Here, the four crosshead handles are mixer controls for the bath and a showerhead above.**

middle row, centre left **This recessed thermostatic shower mixer adjusts the water temperature at the touch of a lever. A similar control from Barber Wilsons with**

a round or square plate and china lever comes in unlacquered brass which will tarnish naturally.

middle row, centre right **This minimal shower wand, part of the Vola suite designed more than 40 years ago by Arne Jacobsen, is a modern classic.**

middle row, near left **A set of period brassware complete with shower mixer, taps and spray is quite a find, but should always be fully refurbished before plumbing in. Similar reproduction sets are available in traditional ranges.**

bottom row, far left **The successor to this modern single-control thermostatic mixer from the Axor range by Hansgrohe is the Aktivated thermostatic shower.**

bottom row, centre left **A shower spray with a ceramic handle often comes as part of a traditional telephone-style bath-shower mixer set like those in the Antique and Georgian ranges by Samuel Heath.**

bottom row, centre right **Genuine antique taps give an air of authenticity to a traditional bathroom. Track down original fittings through antique-bathroom dealers or at architectural salvage yards.**

bottom row, near left **A relaxing drench or an invigorating massage jet – this shower set-up provides both, with a 300 mm Waterloo shower rose by C.P. Hart and an Aktiva showerhead by Hansgrohe that offers a choice of spray patterns.**

opposite, above left **Designed in the 1960s and still in production today, Arne Jacobsen's Vola tap has inspired a whole generation of plumbing fittings. It is minimalist in style with no mechanical parts visible, and there are scores of variations available, including shower fittings, pillar taps and deck- and wall-mounted mixers like this two-handled chrome version with a fixed spout.**

opposite, above right **The indulgence of a freestanding tub is just as appropriate in a modern bathroom as a traditional one – a fact recognized by designers of brassware, who now produce suitably contemporary fittings. This beautifully simple floor-mounted tap is the Vola 090FM. The handles are mounted separately elsewhere.**

opposite, below left **Size and scale should always be taken into consideration when selecting taps. Here a chunky bridge mixer is more in proportion to the extra-large basin it fills than the three-piece mixer or monobloc fitting more commonly used with a smaller bowl.**

opposite, below right **The sculptural three-piece Starck basin mixer with lever handles from the Axor collection by Hansgrohe is well chosen for this console basin, carrying the eye along its width. Like all good designs it works well, the levers being easy to operate with dry or soapy hands.**

above left **Antique chrome taps have a beautiful silvery patina, much softer than the bright gloss of new chrome. Modern finishes that come close to this are satinized chrome and nickel.**

above centre **Salvaged antique bath taps with their worn chrome finish unrestored are a quirky choice for this modern mosaic bath. Although external wear is unimportant, old taps should only be bought if they are in fully working order, as it is hard to find spare parts for them – and skilled engineers willing to repair them are even more elusive.**

above right **Antique taps put the finishing touch to a traditional bathroom, and if you are lucky enough to have inherited them along with the original fittings, they are worth preserving.**

centre right **Strong, simple shapes strike the right note in a contemporary bathroom and few tap designs are more pared-down than the Starck single-lever basin mixer from the Axor range by Hansgrohe. Understated and sculptural, it is specially designed for use on smaller basins.**

below right **Wall-mounted taps have the advantage of leaving the basin rim clear so its shape can be properly appreciated and, more prosaically, it becomes easier to clean. These taps, from the Tara range by Dornbracht, are a contemporary take on the traditional crosshead pattern.**

this page, above left **In this smart limestone bathroom, ducting for the plumbing forms a narrow shelf for toiletries. The mirrored cabinets eliminate the need for a separate looking-glass and visually widen this narrow room.**

this page, above right **A heated towel rail often produces enough heat to warm a small bathroom. The Cobratherm by Bisque is a close alternative to this serpentine chrome towel rail.**

this page, centre right **Wall-mounted glass accessories with chrome or brass fittings are bathroom classics and therefore widely available. More difficult to source are ceramic accessories that form an integral part of the tiling. Longmead Ceramics is one of the few remaining makers.**

this page, below right **Accessories like this chrome towel ring can be found in department stores.**

opposite, above left **Freestanding cabinets are useful in a bathroom with insufficient built-in storage. The reflective surfaces of this piece by Lineabeta (widely available in department stores) are helpful in a small room.**

opposite, above centre **This glass and chrome wall-mounted O.L.C. rack by Agape keeps reading matter tidy in the bathroom.**

opposite, above right **This built-in storage combines cupboards and drawers in a single unit. The drawers pull right out for better access. The idea of aligning the cupboard handles and drawer pulls on one side is a design feature that distinguishes the piece from a store-bought cabinet.**

opposite, below **Built-in furniture packs a lot of storage into a compact space. These cabinets were custom-made in blond birch to match the furniture in the adjoining bedroom and raised on small chrome legs to give a less weighty look. The top, undermounted with a pair of Kohler basins, is made from luminous white Carrara marble.**

storage & accessories

Clutter has a tendency to accumulate in the bathroom, but accessories to hold items in everyday use, combined with well-planned storage for the things you want to display (and the things you would rather hide away) will keep it under control.

Floor-standing bathroom cupboards, wall cabinets and storage trolleys can be found in furniture shops and department stores, but pieces intended for elsewhere in the house can be used just as well in the bathroom provided they will not be damaged by the damp environment. Purpose-made built-in bathroom furniture is becoming more widely available in contemporary and classic styles. Constructed along similar lines to kitchen units, they are sold in modular form so you can create an arrangement to fit your space. Custom-made fitted furniture is usually built in as part of a complete bathroom installation and can be designed as the main feature or cleverly concealed. Whatever the type of storage, in a family bathroom a lockable cupboard or compartment is important for the safe keeping of medicines and sharp items.

Toothbrushes and handtowels need to be kept within reach of where they will be used. For these, wall-mounted fittings are ideal. Perfume bottles, spare soaps and other items that are both decorative and frequently used can be arranged on open shelves.

opposite, above left **Stone can be used successfully for virtually any bathroom surface. For pure elegance choose a pale stone with an interesting grain like this unfilled travertine.**

opposite, above centre **Iroko (a hardwood that can tolerate some moisture) panels the wall behind this bath. Instead of conforming to the usual vertical pattern of wainscoting, a contemporary effect has been achieved by fixing the planks horizontally and leaving regular narrow gaps between them.**

opposite, above right **Concrete is an unlikely choice for a sophisticated bathroom but here a special mix devised by Unique Environments forms the lightly textured, water-resistant walls and smooth steps leading to a sunken bath.**

opposite, centre left **Terrazzo covers the floor and continues up the sides of the bath in this traditional room.**

opposite, centre **Caribbean Mix is the appropriate name for the multi-toned blue mosaic tiles which line this shower area.**

opposite, centre right **Smooth tiles and fine, gritty cement render provide textural contrast in this wet room.**

opposite, below left **Harvey Maria's cork-and-vinyl 'Spring' tiles give the impression of a carpet of roses – a frivolous touch in a tiny bathroom.**

opposite, below centre **Warm grey-brown mussel limestone has narrow, vertical grooves on its horizontal planes in contrast with the smooth, fossil-studded horizontal surfaces.**

opposite, below right **The contrast of fresh green mosaic tiles and the**

natural tones of wood and marble adds a lively note.

below left **These pearly iridescent mosaic tiles form a shimmering surround for a shower area. Similar tiles are available from Fired Earth.**

below centre **Paint of the kind used to coat swimming pools waterproofs the walls of this shower room. Temachlor chlorinated rubber paint by Tikkurila Coatings can be coloured to order.**

below right **Raw, robust waterproof cement render forms a continuous textured surface for the shower wall.**

surface finishes

If a bathroom is to stay looking good, all its surfaces must be moisture tolerant. Floors, shower areas and basin surrounds should be impervious; but walls, furniture and surfaces not in obviously wet areas need only resist occasional splashes of water and the humid atmosphere.

Ceramic tiles and mosaics are traditional surfaces for bathrooms. As long as the grouting is sound, they are completely waterproof and can be used to line a wet room, shower area or even a built-in bath. Natural stone is a favourite for contemporary bathrooms, but to prevent watermarks it is advisable to protect it with a clear seal. Concrete is sometimes used as an alternative to stone. It can be waterproofed by adding the appropriate ingredient during installation and is sometimes surface sealed, too. Some tropical hardwoods, such as teak, can be used in wet areas. Other timbers must be well coated with marine varnish, with joints sealed to prevent moisture penetration. Rubber and vinyl flooring have good water resistance and come in a range of colours and designs, making them a practical and decorative choice.

DIRECTORY

a= above; b = below; c = centre;
l = left; r = right

DOORS & WINDOWS

general & miscellaneous
ECLECTICS
*Contemporary window blinds in
all styles and sliding panels for
doorways.*
Unit 25, Leigh Road
Haine Industrial Estate
Ramsgate CT12 5EU
Tel: 01843 852888
Fax: 01843 853111
info@eclectics.co.uk
www.eclectics.co.uk

FARROW & BALL
*Traditional wallpapers and paints,
including floor paint. International
direct sales and stockists worldwide.*
Uddens Estate
Wimborne BH21 7NL
Tel: 01202 876141
Fax: 01202 873793
farrow-ball@farrow-ball.com
www.farrow-ball.com

traditional & architectural joinery
BRADFORD & SESTINI
*Soft- and hardwood doors and full
range of bespoke period joinery,
such as panelling and staircases.*
The Old Engine House, Hall Farm
Main Street, Kirklington
Newark NG22 8NN
Tel: 01636 816415

JAMES HETLEY
*'Restoration' glass for restoring
period windows.*
Glasshouse Fields
Schoolhouse Lane
London E1 9JA
Tel: 020 7790 2333
Fax: 020 7790 2682

LONDON DOOR COMPANY
*External and interior doors in period
and other styles, plus sash windows.*
153 St John's Hill
London SW11 1TQ
Tel: 020 7801 0877
Fax: 01283 511132

MARVIN ARCHITECTURAL
*Standard-range and bespoke sliding
sash windows and doors.*
Gibbs House
Kennel Road
Ascot SL5 7NT
Tel: 01344 885995
Fax: 01344 885455
www.marvin-architectural.com

TIPTREE JOINERY SERVICES
*Traditional and architectural joinery,
including sash windows and wood
panelling.*
New Road, Tiptree
Colchester CO5 0HQ
Tel: 01621 819220
Fax: 01621 815499

handles, pulls & hardware
ALLGOOD WORLDWIDE
*High-quality contemporary
ironmongery.*
297 Euston Road
London NW1 3AQ
Tel: 0870 609 0009
Fax: 020 7380 1232
info@allgood.co.uk
www.allgood.co.uk
www.allgood.com

HÄFELE
*Huge range of cabinet and furniture
ironmongery.*
www.hafele.com
Available in the UK through:
Swift Valley Industrial Estate
Rugby CV21 1RD
Tel: 01788 542020
Fax: 01788 544440
www.hafele.co.uk

MERIT METAL PRODUCTS
Excellent range of hardware.
242 Valley Road
Warrington PA 18976
USA
Tel: +1 215 343 2500
Fax: +1 215 343 4839
info@meritmetal.com
www.meritmetal.com

NU-LINE
*Shop offering a good range
of hardware.*
317 Westbourne Park Road
London W11 1EF
Tel: 020 7727 7748
Fax: 020 7792 9451

SATURN ARCHITECTURAL
Architectural ironmongery.
Wellington Business Park
Crowthorn RG45 6LS
Tel: 01344 761194
Fax: 01344 762467

VALLI & VALLI LTD
Designer door furniture.
www.vallievalli.com
Available in the UK through:
Unit 6, Viking
Tame Valley Industrial Estate
Tamworth B77 5DU
Tel: 01827 283655
Fax: 01827 280553
vallivalliuk@valli.force9.net

windows
COL-SECURE FACADES LTD
*Supply and install aluminium
windows and shop fronts.*
Secure House
Manders Estate
Old Heath Road
Woverhampton WV1 2RP
Tel: 01902 456667
Fax: 01902 456665
www.col-secure.com

CRITTALL WINDOWS LTD
*Steel windows and doors. Will
replicate period metal windows
for restoration projects.*
Springwood Drive
Braintree CM7 2YN
Tel: 01376 324106
Fax: 01376 349662
hq@crittall-windows.co.uk
www.crittall-windows.co.uk

METAL UK
Windows and conservatories.
Copthall Farm
Breakspeare Road South
Ickenham UB10 8HB
Tel: 01895 629940
Fax: 01895 678811
equiries @metaluk.co.uk
www.metaluk.co.uk

SUNFOLD SYSTEMS
*Folding and sliding doors and
automated rooflights.*
The Greenhouse
93 Norwich Road
East Dereham
Norfolk NR20 3AL
Tel: 01362 699744
Fax: 01362 698787

THE VELUX COMPANY LTD
Woodside Way
Glenrothes East
Fife KY7 4ND
Tel: 01592 772211
www.velux.com

FLOORING

hard flooring
BRITISH CEMENT ASSOCIATION
Provides advice and list of members.
Century House

Telford Avenue
Crowthorne RG45 6YS
Tel: 01344 762676
Fax: 01344 761214
www.bca.org.uk

EMERY & CIE & NOIR D'IVOIRE
Rue de l'Hopital 25-29
Brussels, Belgium
Tel: +32 2513 5892
Fax: +32 2513 3970
gabi.emery@euronet.be

ETERNIT BUILDING MATERIALS LTD
Suppliers of the Brazilian slate p34c.
Whaddon Road
Meldreth
Royston SG8 5RL
Tel: 01763 260421
Fax: 01763 262531
www.eternit.co.uk

FIRED EARTH
*Tiles, wood flooring, natural flooring,
rugs, plus bathrooms. Showrooms
throughout Europe and the Far East.*
Twyford Mill, Oxford Road
Adderbury OX17 3HP
Tel: 01295 814300
Fax: 01295 810832
enquires@firedearth.com
www.firedearth.com

GOODING ALUMINIUM LTD
Aluminium sheet flooring.
1 British Wharf
Landmann Way
London SE14 5RS
Tel: 020 8692 2255
Fax: 020 8469 0031
www.goodingalum.com

GRANITE & MARBLE
INTERNATIONAL LTD
*Supply and installation of natural
stone for floors, walls, countertops,
basins.*
Westminster House
35 Pensbury Place
London SW8 4TR
Tel: 020 7498 2742
Fax: 020 7498 0384
sales@stonework.co.uk
www.stonework.co.uk

LASAR CONTRACTS
*Supply and installation of floor and
wall coatings, including poured
epoxy resin and the marble-and-resin
floor featured p35l,b&c.*
Rougham Industrial Estate
Bury St Edmunds IP30 9ND
Tel: 01359 271417
Fax: 01359 270008
vicmellies@lasarcontracts.ltd.uk
www.lasarcontracts.ltd.uk

LUXOMATION LTD (UK)
Stainless-steel tiles.
Spring Grove Works
579 London Road
Isleworth TW7 4EJ
Tel: 020 8568 6373
Fax: 020 8847 2603
sales@luxomation.com
www.luxomation.com

NATIONAL FEDERATION OF
TERRAZZO, MARBLE & MOSAIC
SPECIALISTS
*Represents contractors and suppliers.
Can advise on projects and provide
details of members.*
PO Box 2843
London W1A 5PG
Tel: 0845 609 0050
Fax: 0845 607 8160
dslade@nftmms.org
www.nftmms.org

PALLAM PRECAST
*Terrazzo, concrete and reconstituted
stone floors (also staircases and
vanity units). Terrazzo tiles similar to
those featured p37a.*
187 West End Lane
London NW6 2LJ
Tel: 020 7328 6512
Fax: 020 7328 3547

PARIS CERAMICS
*Limestone, stone and terracotta
floors, mosaics.*
583 King's Road
London SW6 2EH
Tel: 020 7371 7778
Fax: 020 7371 8395
London@parisceramics.com
www.parisceramics.com

STEVE CHARLES LTD
*Import and install tile, stone,
marble, mosaic and pebble for
floors and walls.*
E1, The Engineering Offices
2 Michael Road
London SW6 2AD
Tel: 020 7384 4424
Fax: 020 7384 4434
sales.stevecharles.com
www.stevecharles.com

STONE AGE LTD
*Limestone and sandstone flooring,
plus washbasins and stone
accessories. Suppliers of the grey
limstone, pietra lara, featured p43b.*
19 Filmer Road
London SW6 7BU
Tel: 020 7385 7954
Fax: 020 7385 7956
info@stone-age.co.uk
www.estone.co.uk

STONELL
Suppliers of natural stone
throughout Europe, including
limestone tiles with keystones similar
to those featured p38bl.
521–525 Battersea Park Road
London SW11 3BN
Tel: 020 7738 9990
Fax: 020 7738 0660
admin@stonell.com
www.stonell.com

TRADSTOCKS
Retailers of natural stone.
Dunaverig, Thornhill
Stirling FK8 3QW
Tel: 01786 850400
Fax: 01786 850404
sales@tradstocks.co.uk
www.tradstocks.co.uk

VILLEROY & BOCH AG
Wall and floor tiles.
P.O.Box 1120
D - 66688 Mettlach, Germany
Tel: +49 6864 81 0
www.villeroy-boch.com
Available in the UK through:
Villeroy & Boch Tiles
Raglans
North End, Ashton Keynes
Swindon SN6 6QR
Tel: 01285 861159
Fax: 01285 861139
fpasqualitto@aol.com

wooden flooring
BERNARD DRU OAK
Traditional oak board floors, parquet
and architectural mouldings.
Bickham Manor
Timberscombe
Minehead TA24 7UA
Tel: 01643 841312
Fax: 01643 841048
info@oakfloor.co.uk
www.oakfloor.co.uk

ENGLISH TIMBERS
Specialist suppliers offering a range
including Canadian maple.
1A Main Street
Kirkburn, Driffield
East Yorkshire YO25 9DU
Tel: 01377 229301
Fax: 01377 229303
www.englishtimbers.co.uk

THE HARDWOOD FLOORING
COMPANY LTD
Will supply and fit over 200 types
of hardwood flooring.
146–152 West End Lane
London NW6 1SD
Tel: 020 7328 8481
Fax: 020 7625 5951
sales@hardwoodflooringcompany.com
www.hardwoodflooringcompany.com

HERITAGE WOODCRAFT LTD
Solid hardwood and wood-block
floors, including end-grain wood
blocks as shown p46ar.
Heritage House
Wheatfield Way
Hinckley LE10 1YG
Tel: 01455 890800
Fax: 01455 890700
sales@woodfloor.co.uk
www.woodfloor.co.uk

JAMES LATHAM PLC
Importer and distributor of timber
and timber products, including the
Wisa spruce ply featured p42b.
Leeside Wharf
Mount Pleasant Hill
London E5 9NG
Tel: 020 8806 3333
Fax: 020 8806 1052
www.lathamtimber.co.uk

JUNCKERS INDUSTRIER A/S
Solid hardwood floors, including
Nordic beech, oak and ash.
Værftsvej
DK-4600 Køge, Denmark
Tel: +45 5665 1895
Fax: +45 5667 3720
junckers@junckers.dk
www.junckers.com
Available in the UK through:
Junckers Ltd
Wheaton Court Commercial Centre
Wheaton Road
Witham CM8 3UJ
Tel: 01376 517512
Fax: 01376 514401
sales/tech@junckers.co.uk
www.junckers.co.uk

KINGSPAN ACCESS FLOORS LTD
Walton House
11–13 The Parade
Leamington Spa CV32 4DG
Tel: 0870 789 4000
Fax: 0870 789 4100
marketing@kingspanaccessfloors.co.uk
mail@kingspan.co.uk (for
international enquiries)
www.kingspanaccessfloors.co.uk

MAFI HOLZVERARBEITUNG GMBH
A-5212, Schneegattern 7
Austria
Tel: +43 7746 2711
Fax: +43 7746 3747
office@mafi.at
www.mafi.co.at
Available in the UK through:
Element 7
Unit 2, Parsons Green Depot
Parsons Green Lane
London SW6 4HH
Tel: 020 7736 2366
Fax: 020 7736 2468
sales@element7.co.uk

OSMO (UK) LTD
Solid wood, plankwood, block strip,
laminate and cork tile floors.
Unit 2, Stocklake Industrial Estate
Pembroke Road
Aylesbury HP20 1DB
Tel: 01296 481220
Fax: 01296 424090
osmo@btconnect.com
www.osmouk.com

SOLOPARK PLC
Reclamation yard. Oak and
hardwood floorings. Woodblock
floorings in pine, oak, beech
and mahogany, similar to that
featured p43al.
Station Road
Near Pampisford CB2 4HB
Tel: 01223 834663
Fax: 01223 834780
info@solopark.co.uk
www.solopark.co.uk

UPM-KYMMENE WOOD PRODUCTS
INDUSTRY
Wisa wood.
P.O. Box 380
00101 Helsinki, Finland
Tel: +358 204 15 111
Fax: +358 204 15 0388

floor paints
FARROW & BALL
(See Doors & Windows)

PLASCON INTERNATIONAL
Special-purpose paints including
paints for various floor surfaces,
including colourful paints such as
that featured p49al.
Brewery House
High Street, Twyford
Winchester SO211RG
Tel: 01962 717001/2
Fax: 01962 711503
info@plascon.co.uk
www.plascon.co.uk

sheet & soft tile
BILL AMBERG
Leather flooring.
10 Chepstow Road
London W2 5BD
Tel: 020 7727 3560
Fax: 020 7727 3541
mail@billambergshop.com
www.billamberg.com

DALSOUPLE
Rubber floors and other surfaces.
PO Box 140
Bridgwater TA5 1HT
Tel: 01984 667233
Fax: 01984 667366
info@dalsouple.com
www.dalsouple.com

FIRST FLOOR (FULHAM) LTD
Suppliers of rubber, linoleum and
vinyl flooring, including the textured
vinyl featured p53bl.
174 Wandsworth Bridge Road
London SW6 2UQ
Tel: 020 7736 1123

FORBO INTERNATIONAL SA
Marmoleum and cushioned vinyl.
8193 Eglisau
Zurich, Switzerland
Tel: +41 1 868 2525
info@forbo.com
www.forbo.com
Available in the UK through:
Forbo-Nairn
PO Box 1, Den Road
Kircaldy, Fife KY1 2SB
Tel: 0800 731 2369
Fax: 01592 643999
headoffice@forbo-linoleum.co.uk
www.marmoleum.co.uk

LASER CONTRACTS
Poured epoxy floors.
(See Hard Flooring)

MARMOLEUM
(See Forbo-Nairn)

SINCLAIR TILL
Linoleum custom-made with inlaid
designs, as featured p52al.
791–793 Wandsworth Road
London SW8 3JQ
Tel: 020 7720 0031
Fax: 020 7498 3814.

TREADMASTER
Anti-slip flooring in rubber-bonded
cork.
Tiflex Ltd, Tiflex House
Liskeard PL14 4NB
Tel: 01579 320808
Fax: 01579 320802
liskeard@tiflex.co.uk
www.tiflex.co.uk

natural fibres & carpets
CHRISTINE VANDERHURD
Custom-designed handwoven,
machine-made and tufted rugs
and carpets.
Postal address:
Studio 276, 56 Gloucester Road
London SW7 4UB
Tel: 020 7313 5400
Fax: 020 7229 7776
christine@christinevanderhurd.com
www.christinevanderhurd.com

CHRISTOPHER FARR
Handmade contemporary rugs.
212 Westbourne Grove
London W11 2RH
Tel: 020 7792 5761
Fax: 020 7792 5763

info@cfarr.co.uk
www.cfarr.co.uk

CRUCIAL TRADING
Natural flooring, rugs and runners,
including herringbone coir similar
to p54ar.
PO Box 11, Duke Place
Kidderminster DY10 2JR
Tel: 01562 825656
Fax: 01562 820030

HELEN YARDLEY
Hand-tufted rugs and wall hangings.
A/Z Studios, 3/5 Hardwidge Street
London SE1 3SY
Tel: 020 7403 7114
Fax: 020 7403 8906
info@helenyardley.com
www.helenyardley.com

JOHN LEWIS
Oxford Street
London W1A 1EX
Tel: 020 7629 7711
www.johnlewis.com

ROGER OATES DESIGN
Rugs and runners in contemporary
designs, textured finishes, neutral
flatweave and Wiltons.
The Long Barn, Eastnor
Ledbury HR8 1EL
Tel: 01531 631611
Fax: 01531 631 361
shop@rogeroates.com
www.rogeroates.com

STARK CARPET
Carpets and rugs.
3/6–7 Chelsea Harbour Design Centre
Chelsea Harbour, Lots Road
London SW10 OXE
Tel: 020 7352 6001
starkcarpet@btconnect.com
www.starkcarpet.com

WALLS & CEILINGS
(See Doors & Windows for traditional
and architectural joinery)

ARMOURCOAT SURFACE FINISHES
Decorative polished plaster finishes.
Morewood Close
London Road
Sevenoaks TN13 2HU
Tel: 01732 460668
Fax: 01732 450930
sales@armourcoat.co.uk
www.armourcoat.com

BILHUBER BASICS
Bilhuber Inc.
3330 East 59th Street, 6th Floor
New York NY 10022
USA
Tel: +1 212 308 4888

DIRECTORY

DIRECTORY

CAPITAL CRISPIN VENEER
Large selection of wood veneers.
Unit 12, Bow Industrial Park
Carpenters Road
London E15 2DZ
Tel: 020 8525 0300
Fax: 020 8525 0070
www.jcrispinandsons.co.uk

D & N PRODUCTS
Makers of leather panels featured p72l.
Tel: 020 8695 5686

GRAHAM & BROWN
Wallcoverings including blown vinyl in contemporary designs.
P.O. Box 39, India Mill
Harwood Street
Blackburn BB1 3DB
Tel: 01254 691321
Fax: 01254 291001
export@grahambrown.com
www.grahambrown.com

KENFIELD
Suppliers of metal fittings used for leather panels p72l.
Tel: 0121 451 3051
www.kenfield.com

LUXCRETE
UK distributor of glass blocks for domestic and commercial use. Products featured p61ar and p161br.
Premier House, Disraeli Road
London NW10 7BT
Tel: 020 8965 7292
Fax: 020 8961 6337
www.luxcrete.co.uk

MARMODECOR
Supplier of travertine, marble and other decorative stone.
C9A The Chambers
Chelsea Harbour
London SW10 0XF
Tel: 020 7351 3700
Fax: 020 7351 2700

PAPERS & PAINTS
Paint specialist with excellent range of historical colours and off whites. International mail-order service.
4 Park Walk
London SW10 0AD
Tel: 020 7352 8626
Fax: 020 7352 1017
enquiries@papers-paints.co.uk
www.papers-paints.co.uk

PRIVA-LITE
Electrically switchable obscured glass.
www.sggprivalite.com
Available in the UK through:
Solaglas Ltd
Clipper Boulevard East

Crossways
Dartford DA2 6QN
Tel: 01322 297 674
Fax: 01322 297 651

SOLARIS GLASS BRICKS
Siemensstraße 1
D-56422 Wirges
Germany
Tel: +49 2602 681-0
Fax: +49 2602 681-425
info.solaris-glasstein@saint-gobain.com
info-export.solaris-glasstein@saint-gobain.com
www.solaris-glasstein.de
Available in the UK through:
H.W. Cooper & Co
Page House
33 Pages Walk
London SE1 4SF
Tel: 020 7237 1767

TIMBNET
Distributor of iroko and other hardwoods.
235 Bagmoor Road
Shieldhall
Glasgow G51 4SH
Tel: 0141 440 0060
Fax: 0141 445 5736

TIMOROUS BEASTIES
Wallcoverings including bespoke and Op-art designs
7 Craigend Place
Glasgow G13 2UN
Tel: 0141 959 3331
Fax: 0141 959 8880
www.timorousbeasties.com

STAIRCASES

(See Doors & Windows for traditional and architectural joinery)

ALBION DESIGN OF CAMBRIDGE
Cast-iron and steel spiral staircases in traditional and modern designs.
Unit H3, Dales Manor Business Park
Babraham Road
Sawston CB2 4TJ
Tel: 01223 836128
Fax: 01223 837117
sales@albionspirals.co.uk
www.albionspirals.co.uk

BISCA DESIGN
Bespoke contemporary ironwork for staircases.
Sawmill Lane
Helmsley YO62 5DQ
Tel: 01439 771702
Fax: 01439 771002
info@bisca.co.uk
www.bisca.co.uk

RICHARD BURBIDGE LTD
Standard and bespoke timber stair balustrading.
Whittington Road
Oswestry SY11 1HZ
Tel: 01691 655131
Fax: 01691 657694
info@richardburbidge.co.uk
www.richardburbidge.co.uk

E.A. HIGGINSON & CO
Straight and spiral timber staircases made to order.
Unit 1, Carlisle Road
London NW9 0HD
Tel: 020 8200 4848
Fax: 020 8200 8249
sales@higginson.co.uk
www.higginson.co.uk

SAFETY STAIRWAYS LTD
Reproduction Victorian cast-iron and contemporary stainless-steel spiral staircases.
Unit 45, Owen Road Industrial Estate
Owen Road
Willenhall WV13 2PX
Tel: 0121 526 3133
Fax: 0121 526 2833

SPIRAL STAIRCASE SYSTEMS
Standard-system and fully bespoke contemporary staircases made from wood, metal, glass or acrylic.
Lewes Design Contracts Ltd
The Mill
Glynde BN8 6SS
Tel: 01273 858 341
Fax: 01273 858 200
spiral@pavilion.co.uk
www.spiralstairs.co.uk

HEATING

general & miscellaneous

GAROUSTE & BONETTI AT DAVID GILL GALLERIES
Contemporary decorative furniture.
(See Lighting)

THE STONE FEDERATION OF GREAT BRITAIN
Information about quarries and stone masons.
Construction House
56–64 Great Leonard Street
London EC2A 4JX
Tel: 020 7608 5094
Fax: 020 7608 5081

WIDNEY
Telescopic slides.
Plume Street
Aston
Birmingham B6 7SA
Tel: 0121 327550

Fax: 0121 282466
www.widney.co.uk

fireplaces, surrounds & grates

THE ARTS & CRAFTS HOME
Reproduction Arts and Crafts furniture and accessories including some fireplaces.
28 Gloucester Road, North Laines
Brighton BN1 4AQ
Tel: 01273 600073
www.achome.co.uk

CHESNEY'S
Antique and new fireplaces in marble, stone and wood and a range of grates.
194–202 Battersea Park Road
London SW11 4ND
Tel: 020 7627 1410
Fax: 020 7622 1078
sales@antiquefireplace.co.uk
www.antiquefireplace.co.uk

CVO FIREVAULTS
Range of contemporary gas fires and special commissions.
36 Great Titchfield Street
London W1P 7AD
Tel: 020 7580 5333
Fax: 020 7255 2234
info@cvo.co.uk
www.cvo.co.uk

ELGIN & HALL
Modern and traditional fireplaces in simulated stone in a range of matt, metallic and stone finishes. Also produce and inset fires.
Adelphi House
Hunton, Bedale
North Yorkshire DL8 1LY
Tel: 01677 450100
Fax: 01677 450713
sales@elgin.co.uk
www.elgin.co.uk

GAZCO LTD
Makers of flame-effect gas fires and stoves including modern inset and Victorian reproduction fireplaces. Also offer made to measure service.
Osprey Road
Sowton Industrial Estate
Exeter EX2 7JG
Tel: 01392 444030
Fax: 01392 444148
info@gazco.com
www.gazco.com

PLATONIC FIREPLACE COMPANY
Produce unusual contemporary flame-effect gas fires with ceramic 'Geolog' 3-dimensional shapes, pebbles and rocks instead of coals, similar to the fire featured on p92.
Phoenix Wharf, Eel Pie Island

Twickenham TW1 3DY
Tel: 020 8891 5904
Fax: 020 8892 2590
platonicfireplace@btinternet.com
www.platonicfireplaces.co.uk

R.C. COPPIN & SON
Monumental masons. Built fireplace featured p91ar.
Unit 2, Park Drive Industrial Estate
Braintree CN7 1AP
Tel: 01376 550009

STONEWORKS
Make fireplace surrounds to order and in any suitable stone.
42 Colville Road
London W3 8BL
Tel: 020 8993 2118
Fax: 020 8993 3511
www.stoneworks-uk.com

TOWNSEND'S
Antique and reproduction fireplaces in wood, marble, stone and cast iron. Makers of the fire surround featured p91 al.
81 Abbey Road
London NW8 0AE
Tel: 020 7624 4756

radiators & heating systems

BISQUE
(See Bathrooms)

CLYDE COMBUSTIONS LTD
Column and tubular steel radiators and towel rails.
Cox Lane
Chessington KT9 1SL
Tel: 020 8391 2020
Fax: 020 8397 4598
www.clyde4heat.co.uk

GUNNING ENGINEERING LTD
Tubular radiators, trench heating and grilles.
Unit 8, Robert Way
Wickford SS11 8DD
Tel: 070 41 351 313
Fax: 070 41 351 314
www.gunning-heating-products.co.uk

JAGA INTERNATIONAL
Trench heaters, tubular, panel radiators and bathroom radiators.
Tel: +32 11 29 41 16
sales@jaga.be
www.the radiatorfactory.com
Available in the UK through:
Jaga Heating Products (UK)
Jaga House, Orchard Business Park
Bromyard Road
Ledbury HR8 1LG
Tel: 01531 631533
Fax: 01531 631534
jaga@jaga.co.uk

MHS RADIATORS LTD
Cast-iron column radiators in traditional and reproduction Victorian designs. The columns are made individually, so almost any length can be achieved. Flat-fronted radiators and towel rails.
35 Nobel Square
Burnt Mills Industrial Estate
Basildon SS13 1LT
Tel: 01268 591010
Fax: 01268 728202
info@mhsdirect.com
www.mhsdirect.com

THERMIC
Horizontal and vertical rail radiators.
Heulentakstraat z/n
B-3650 Dilsen, Belgium
Tel: +32 89 790444
Fax: +32 89 790555
www.thermic.be
Available in the UK through:
KV Services
5 Main Road
Kilsby
Rugby CV23 8XR
Tel: 01788 823286
Fax: 01788 823002

ZEHNDER
Column and panel radiators and towel rails.
Moortalstrasse 1
Postfach CH-5722 Gränichen
Switzerland
Tel: +41 62 855 15 00
info@zehnder.net
Available in the UK through:
B15 Armstrong Mall
Southwood Business Park
Farnborough GU14 0NR
Tel: 01252 531200
Fax: 01252 531201
www.zehnder.co.uk

stoves

ESSE STOVES
Heating and cooking stoves. Matt-black and enamelled stoves including some reproduction Art Nouveau designs. Models similar to that featured p102 al.
Ouzledale Foundry Co Ltd
Long Ing, Barnoldswick
Lancashire BB18 6BN
Tel: 01282 813235
Fax: 01282 816876
esse@ouzledale.co.uk
www.ouzledale.co.uk

FLAMEWAVE FIRES
Floor-standing stoves and inset fires similar to that featured p93 ar.
The Cold Store
Pearsons Green, Brenchley
Tonbridge TN12 7DE
Tel: 01892 724458

Fax: 01892 724966
info@flamewavefires.co.uk
www.flamewavefires.co.uk

MORSØ
Scandinavian cast-iron stoves.
Furvej 9
7900 Nykøbing Mors, Denmark
Tel: +45 9669 1900
stoves@morsoe.com
www.morsoe.com
Available in the UK through:
Morsø
Wood Lane, Erdington
Birmingham B24 9QP
Tel: 0121 386 6306
www.morsostoves.co.uk

RAIS A/S
Wood burning and multi-fuel stoves.
Industrivej 20, Vangen
DK-9900 Frederikshaven
Denmark
www.rais.dk
Available in the UK through:
Art of Fire
Tel: 01865 326364
www.rais.co.uk

VERMONT CASTINGS
410 Admiral Boulevard
Mississauga
Ontario L5T 2N6, Canada
Tel: +1 905 670 7777
Fax: +1 905 670 4676
www.vermontcastings.com
Available in the UK through:
CFM Kinder Ltd
Trentham Lakes
Stoke-on-Trent
Staffordshire ST4 4TJ
Tel: 01782 339000
Fax: 01782 339009

WARRIOR STOVES
Distributors of multi-fuel stoves, including the Air-tight Box Heater, similar to that featured p103 ar.
Chapel Road
Tuckingmill
Camborne TR14 8QX
Tel: 01209 715500
Fax: 01209 612322

YEOMAN STOVES
Wood, multi-fuel, gas- and oil-burning cast-iron and steel stoves in traditional styles. Models similar to that featured p102 al.
Sidmouth Road
Clyst St Mary EX5 1BP
Tel: 013952 34567
Fax: 01395 234568
sales@yeoman-stoves.co.uk
www.yeoman-stoves.co.uk

STORAGE

ARMANI CASA MILANO
Christian Biecher is the designer for the new Armani Casa collection.
Via Manzoni, 31
Milan 20121, Italy
Tel: +39 272 31 86 30
Fax: +39 272 31 86 39
www.armanicasa.com

CALIFORNIA CLOSETS
Contemporary custom-made storage for wardrobes, utility rooms and other areas.
227 King's Road
London SW3 5EJ
Tel: 0845 606 6063
Fax: 020 7376 7767
www.calclosets.co.uk

GLAVERBEL UK
Producer of Colorbel opaque frit-enamelled glass.
Chestnut Field
Regent Place
Rugby CV21 2TL
Tel: 01788 535353
www.glaverbel.be

HOLLY HUNT
Supplier of Christain Liagre wall sconces featured p110b.
150 E 58th Street
New York NY10155
USA
Tel +1 212-891-2500
Fax +1 212-891-2599
www.hollyhunt.com

HÜLSTA
Fitted-look freestanding furniture for living rooms, bedrooms and children's rooms.
22 Bruton Street
London W1X 7DA
Tel: 020 7629 4881
Fax: 020 7409 2417
sales.enquiries@huelsta.co.uk
www.huelsta.co.uk

IKEA
Inexpensive but stylish freestanding storage furniture for every room.
2 Drury Way
North Circular Road
London NW10 0TH
Tel: 020 8208 5600
www.IKEA.co.uk

INTERLÜBKE
Sleek contemporary storage for bedrooms and living rooms.
Gebr. Lubke GmbH & Co KG
D-33378 Rheda-Widenbruck
Germany
Tel: +49 52 42/12-1
Fax: +49 52 42/12-206

www.interluebke.de
Available in the UK through:
ZPC Agencies
Interlubke London
P.O. Box 13990
London SE14 5WP
Tel: 020 7207 4710
Fax: 020 7207 4744

LIGNE ROSET
Modern storage furniture and accessories for the living room, bedroom and hall.
Roset (U.K.) Ltd
High Street
Great Missenden HP16 0AL
Tel: 01494 865001
Fax: 01484 866883
www.ligne-roset.co.uk

NEOTU
Design company featuring furniture designed by Christian Biecher.
545 W34 Street, Suite 3C
New York NY10001
USA
Tel: +1 212 695 9404
neotunyc@neotu.com
www.neotu.com

PERSPEX
(See Bathrooms)

PUNT MOBLES S.L.
Maker of the Literatura shelving system.
Islas Baleares, 48
46988 Fuente del Jarro
Valencia, Spain
Tel: +34 96 1343270
Fax: +34 96 134268
puntmobles@puntmobles.es
www.puntmobles.es

SELFRIDGES
Contemporary furnishings.
400 Oxford Street
London W1A 1AB
Tel: 020 7629 1234
Fax: 020 7495 8321
www.selfridges.co.uk

VITSOE
Classic 20th-century modern shelving. Distribute internationally from London offices.
Tel: 020 7354 8444
Fax: 020 7354 9888
details@vitsoe.com
www.vitsoe.com

LIGHTING

ANGLEPOISE
Unit 51, Enfield Industrial Area
Redditch B97 6DR
Tel: 01527 63771

Fax: 01527 61232
sales@anglepoise.co.uk
www.anglepoise.co.uk

ARTELUCE
(See Flos)

ARTEMIDE GB
Contemporary architectural, domestic, decorative and task lighting.
106 Great Russell Street
London WC1B 3NB
Tel: 020 7631 5200
Fax: 020 7631 5222
info@artemide.co.uk
www.artemide.com

BEST & LLOYD
Traditional brass lighting, and 'Bestlite' range.
Lycourt, 1a Ampton Road
Edgebaston
Birmingham B15 2UP
Tel: 0121 558 1191
Fax: 0121 565 3547
www.bestandlloyd.co.uk

BOX PRODUCTS LTD
Design and production of lighting, furniture and clocks to architects, interior designers and private clients.
3 Russell House
Cambridge Street
London SW1V 4EQ
Tel: 020 7401 2288
Fax: 020 7828 7133
boxproducts@btinternet.com

BOYD LIGHTING
Architectural lighting and handcrafted designs.
944 Folsom Street
San Francisco CA 94107-1007
USA
Tel: +1 415 778 4300
Fax: +1 415 778 4319
info@boydlighting.com
www.boydlighting.com

CHARLOTTE PACKE
Lighting consultant and designer, one-off designs and some retail.
C.P.D.
26 A The Avenue
London NW6 7YD
charlottepacke@yahoo.co.uk

CHRISTOPHER WRAY LIGHTING
591–593 King's Road
London SW6 2YW
Tel: 020 7751 8703
Fax: 020 7751 8704
www.christopherwray.co.uk

DIRECTORY

THE CONRAN SHOP
Furniture shops with good contemporary lighting.
Michelin House
81 Fulham Road
London SW3 6RD
Tel: 020 7589 7401
Fax: 020 7823 7015
fulham@conranshop.co.uk
www.conranshop.co.uk

DAVID GILL GALLERIES
20th-century and contemporary furniture; Serge Mouille lighting.
60 Fulham Road
London SW3 6HH
Tel: 020 7589 5946
Fax: 020 7584 9184
info@davidgillgalleries.co.uk

ERCO LEUCHTEN GMBH
Brockhauser Weg 80-82
D-58507 Lüdenscheid
Tel: +49 2351 551 0
Fax: +49 2351 551 300
info@erco.com
www.erco.com
Available in the UK through:
Erco Lighting Ltd
38 Dover Street
London W1S 4NL
Tel: 020 7408 0320
Fax: 020 7409 1530
info.uk@erco.com

FLOS
Contemporary lighting, including work of designers Jasper Morrison, Philippe Starck, A & PG Castiglioni and others. Encompasses the Arteluce range.
www.flos.net
Available in the UK through:
McInnes Cook
31 Lisson Grove
London NW1 6UB
Tel: 020 7258 0600
Fax: 020 7723 7005

FORBES & LOMAX LTD
205B St John's Hill
London SW11 1TH
Tel: 020 7738 0202
Fax: 020 7738 9224
sales@forbesandlomax.co.uk
www.forbesandlomax.co.uk

4 DESK TABLE LAMPS AND SHADES
Reproduction lighting in Art Nouveau and Tiffany styles.
POB 25, Stewartsville NJ 08886
USA
Tel: +1 908 479 4614
Fax: +1 908 479 6158
lamps@4-collectors.com
www.timelesslamps.com

HABITAT
Furniture shop with inexpensive modern lighting, including pendant lights similar to p127r; Soho 2000 is similar to lamp featured p129br.
196 Tottenham Court Road
London W1P 9LD
Tel: 0845 6010740
Fax: 020 7255 6043
customerrelations@habitat.co.uk
www.habitat.net

HECTOR FINCH LIGHTING
Excellent range of of period and reproduction decorative lighting from 1900 to present day.
88–90 Wandsworth Bridge Road
London SW6 2TF
Tel: 020 7731 8886
Fax: 020 7731 7408
hector@hectorfinch.com
www.hectorfinch.com

HISTORIC LIGHTING INC
Wide range of Arts and Crafts lighting.
114 East Lemon Avenue
Monrovia CA 91016
USA
Tel: +1 626 303 4899
Fax: +1 626 358 6159
www.historiclighting.com

HOMEIER KUCHENTECHNIK GMBH
Kitchen extractors and lighting.
Lichtenfelser Strasse 9
93057 Regensburg, Germany
Tel: +49 941 69 68 30
hreinhold@homeier.com
www.homeier.com
Available in the UK through:
Fulham Kitchens
19 Carnwarth Road
London SW6 3HR
Tel: 020 7736 6458
Fax: 020 7371 0254

IGUZZINI ILLUMINAZIONE S.R.L.
s.s.77.Km102
62019 Recanati-MC, Italy
Tel: +39 071 758 81
Fax: +39 071 758 8295
iguzzini@iguzzi.it
www.iguzzini.com
Available in the UK through:
IGuzzini Illuminazione UK Ltd
Unit 3, Mitcham Industrial Estate
85 Streatham Road
Mitchan CR4 2AP
Tel: 020 8646 4141
Fax: 020 8640 6910
info@iguzzini.co.uk
iguzzini.co.uk

IKEA
Furniture shop selling budget contemporary lighting.
(See Storage)

ISAMU NOGUCHI GARDEN MUSEUM STORE
Lighting, furniture, books and videos.
The Isamu Noguchi Foundation
36-01 43rd Avenue @36th Street
Long Island City
Queens NY 11101
USA
Tel: +1 718 204 7088
Fax: +1 718 278 2348
akari@noguchi.org
www.noguchi.org

JOHN CULLEN LIGHTING
Discreet lighting for the house and garden.
585 King's Road
London SW6 2EH
Tel: 020 7371 5400
Fax: 020 7371 7799
sales@johncullenlighting.co.uk
www.johncullenlighting.co.uk

LIGHTING COLLABORATIVE
Suppliers of Electro Track lighting.
124 West 24th
New York, NY 10011
USA
Tel: +1 212 627 5330

LONDON LIGHTING CO.
Contemporary European lighting.
135 Fulham Road
London SW3 6RT
Tel: 020 7589 3612
Fax: 020 7581 9652

LOUIS POULSEN
Contemporary and modern classic lighting by Poul Heningsen, Arne Jacobsen, Verner Panton and others.
Nyhavn 11
Postboks 7, 1001 Kobenhavn K
Denmark
Tel: +45 33 14 14 114
Fax: +45 33 14 17 10
www.louis-poulsen.dk
Available in the UK through:
Louis Poulsen UK
Surrey Business Park
Weston Road
Epson KT17 1JG
Tel: 01372 848 800
Fax: 01372 848 801
info@ols.co.uk
louis-poulsen.co.uk

LUMESS AG
Contemporary light fittings.
Binningerstrasse 101
4123 Allschwil, Switzerland
Tel: +41 61 481 0066
Fax: +41 61 481 9929
Available in the UK through:
Heal's
196 Tottenham Court Road
London W1P 9LD

Tel: 020 7636 1666
Fax: 020 7637 5582
www.heals.co.uk

LUTRON ELECTRONICS CO.
Lighting controls.
7200 Suter Road
Coopersburg PA18036
Tel: +1 610 282 3800
product@lutron.com
www.lutron.com

MATHMOS
Lava lamps and other innovative lighting.
20–24 Old Street
London EC1V 9AP
Tel: 020 7549 2710
Fax: 020 7549 2715
mathmos@mathmos.com
www.mathmos.com

MAX WATT DESIGN
Contemporary wooden lamps and shades in grasscloth, cork and wood veneer.
Unit 21, Wellesley Road
Tharston Industrial Estate
Long Stratton NR15 2PD
Tel/fax: 01508 532545

THE MICA LIGHT COMPANY
Reproduction Arts & Crafts lamps.
517 State Street
Glendale CA 91203
USA
Tel: +1 818 241 7227
Fax: +1 818 241 5839
sales@micalamps.com
www.micalamps.com

OPTELMA LIGHTING
Low-voltage track lighting and mains-voltage fittings.
14 Napier Court, The Science Park
Abingdon OX14 3NB
Tel: 01235 553769
Fax: 01235 523005
sales@optelma.co.uk
www.optelma.co.uk

PHILIPS LIGHTING UK
The Philips Centre
420–430 London Road
Croydon CR9 3QR
Tel: 020 8665 6655
Fax: 020 8684 0136
www.philips.com

R. HAMILTON & CO LTD
Switches, sockets, dimmers.
Quarry Industrial Estate
Mere BA12 6LA
Tel: 01747 860088
Fax: 01747 861032
info@hamilton-litestat.com
www.hamilton-litestat.com

SERGE MOUILLE
(See David Gill Galleries)

SKK
Innovative lighting consultants and designers of fittings and switches.
34 Lexington Street
London W1F 0LH
Tel: 020 7434 4095
Fax: 020 7287 0168
skk@easynet.co.uk
www.skk.net

STEVEN AMIN
Acid-etched and brilliant-cut glass. Victorian stained-glass reproduction Tiffany lamps.
Glaziers and Stained Glass Studio
14–16 St Ronans Road
Monkseaton
Whitley Bay
Tyne & Wear NE25 8AY
Tel/fax: 0191 251 4893
info@stained-glass-studio.co.uk
www.stained-glass-studio.co.uk

STRICTLY MISSION
Internet supplier of Arts and Crafts furniture and lighting including Frank Lloyd Wright designs.
www.strictlymission.com

TALLER UNO SA
Range of contemporary table, floor, wall and pendant lighting. UK distribution through Optelma.
Balmes 11, 17465 Camallera
Girona, Spain
Tel: +34 972 79 41 27
Fax: +34 972 79 43 13
info@talleruno.com
www.talleruno.com

A TOUCH OF BRASS
Products similiar to the bronze-finished switches p135bc.
210 Fulham Road
London SW10 9PJ
Tel: 020 7351 2255
Fax: 020 7352 4682

WANDSWORTH GROUP
Electrical manufacturers of switches, switchplates and sockets, including the Series 2 4-gang switchplate like that featured p134; will also custom-make banks of switches, including plates of dimmer controls.
Albert Drive
Sheerwater
Woking GU21 5SE
Tel: 01483 740740
Fax: 01483 740384
marketing@wandsworthgroup.com
www.wandsworthgroup.com

UNIQUE INTERIEUR
Kalkbrænderiløbskaj 4
dk-2100 Copenhagen, Denmark
Tel: +45 30 20 02 33
Fax: +45 30 20 02 56
design@uniqueinterieur.dk
www.uniqueinterieur.com

KITCHENS

units & surfaces

ALNO UK
Unit 10, Hampton Farm Industrial
Estate
Hampton Road
West Hanworth TW13 6DB
Tel: 020 8898 4781
www.alno.co.uk

BULTHAUP
Cutting-edge kitchens.
37 Wigmore Street
London W1U 1PN
Tel: 020 7495 3663
www.bulthaup.com

CARRON PHOENIX LTD
*Kitchen sinks in stainless steel,
ceramic and reconstituted quartz;
also taps, including the Pinto model,
similar to p147t. Dealers worldwide.*
Carron Works
Stenhouse Road
Falkirk FK2 8DW
Tel: 01324 638 321
Fax: 01324 620 978
fgp-sales@carron.com
www.carron.com

CAST ADVANCED CONCRETES
*Produce ready-made polished and
sealed concrete worksurfaces.*
Unit 4, Rempstone Barns
Corfe Castle
Wareham BH20 5JH
Tel: 01929 480757
cast.ac@virgin.net

CORIAN®
*A mineral- and acrylic-based material
for worksurfaces and sinks in a
choice of over 100 colours.*
DuPont Corian®
McD Marketing
Maylands Ave
Hemel Hempstead HP2 7DP
Tel: 0800 962116
Fax: 01442 346755
www.corian.co.uk

EDGAR UDNY
*Mosaic and swimming-pool tiles.
Suppliers of tiles featured p142br.*
314 Balham High Road
London SW17 7AA
Tel: 020 8767 8181
Fax: 020 8767 7709

FEENY
*Kitchen and bathroom storage,
shelving, speciality fittings.*
Knape & Vogt Manufacturing Co.
270 Oak Industrial Drive NE
Grand Rapids MI 49505
USA
Tel: +1 616 459 3311
Fax: +1 616 459 3467
postmstr@kv.com
www.kv.com
Available in the UK through:
Unico Components Ltd
101 Walnut Tree Close
Guildford GU1 4UQ
Tel: 01483 577545
Fax: 01483 506987

FORMICA
*Laminates for kitchen units,
worktops and bathroom vanity units,
plus commercial applications.*
Coast Road, North Shields
Tyne & Wear NE29 8RE
Tel: 0191 259 3000
Fax: 0191 258 2719
www.@formica-europe.com

FORMICA PSM
*Impress special-order service for
screen printing bespoke designs on
laminate.*
Aycliffe Industrial Park
Newton Aycliffe
County Durham DL5 6EF
Tel: 01325 303353
Fax: 01325 303348
david.downs@formica-europe.com
www.formica-europe.com

FS MARBLE & GRANITE LTD
*Producers of granite and marble
worktops.*
The Slough
Studley B80 7EN
Tel: 01527 852 717
Fax: 01527 850490
www.fsmarbleandgranite.co.uk

FULHAM KITCHENS
(See Lighting)

GEC ANDERSON
*Custom-made stainless-steel sinks
and worktops, incorporating
cabinets, drawers and shelving.*
Oakengrove, Shire Lane
Hastoe HP23 6LY
Tel: 01442 826999
Fax: 01442 825999
email@gecanderson.co.uk
www.gecanderson.co.uk

GRANITE AND MARBLE
INTERNATIONAL
(See Hard Flooring)

IKEA
*Furnishing store selling kitchen units
and furniture.*
(See Storage)

JOHNNY GREY
Kitchen designer.
Fyning Copse, Rogate
Petersfield GU31 5DH
Tel: 01730 821424
www.johnnygrey.co.uk

PLAIN ENGLISH
Traditional custom-made kitchens.
The Tannery, Combs
Stowmarket IP14 2EN
Tel: 01449 774028

POGGENPOHL
*Contemporary German kitchen
design.*
Lloyds Court
681–685 Silbury Boulevard
Milton Keynes MK9 3AZ
Tel: 0800 243781
kitchens@poggenpohl-group.co.uk
www.poggenpohl.de

RHODE DESIGN
Bespoke kitchens.
137–139 Essex Road
London N1 2NR
Tel: 020 7354 9933

STONE AGE LTD
*Suppliers of stone, including
the pietro laro beige limestone
on p139cl.*
(See Hard Flooring)

UK MARBLE
*Producers of granite and marble
worktops.*
21 Burcott Road
Hereford BS24 9LW
Tel: 01432 352178
Fax: 01432 352 112

taps & plumbing

ATRIFLO
*Traditional and contemporary
kitchen taps; monobloc, three-hole
and pillar styles. Bib taps similar to
those featured p146ac, and the
Phoenician mixer tap which is similar
to that p146bc.*
Avilion Ltd
Orwell Close
Fairview Industrial Park
Rainham RM13 8UB
Tel: 01708 526361
Fax: 01708 550220
sales@avilion.co.uk
www.avilion.co.uk

BARBER WILSONS & CO LTD
*Kitchen and laboratory taps and
bathroom and shower fittings,*

*including models similar to that
featured p149tr.*
Crawley Road, Wood Green
London N22 6AH
Tel: 020 8888 3461
Fax: 020 8888 2041
sales@barwil.co.uk
www.barwil.co.uk

BRASS & TRADITIONAL SINKS
Export internationally.
Devauden Green
Chepstow NP16 6PL
Tel: 01291 650743
Fax: 01291 650827
info@sinks.co.uk
www.sinks.co.uk.

BRISTAN LTD
*Kitchen and bathroom taps, shower
fittings and bathroom accessories.
International exports.*
Lagrange
Lichfield Road Industrial Estate
Tamworth B79 7XD
Tel: 01827 68525
Fax: 01827 68553
orders@bristan.com
www.bristan.com

DORNBRACHT
*Kitchen and bathroom taps and
bathroom accessories.*
Armaturenfabrik
Kobbingser Muhle 6
D-58640 Iserlohn, Germany
Tel: +49 2371 4330
Fax: +49 2371 433135
mail@dornbracht.de
www.dornbracht.de
Available in the UK through:
Splash Distribution
Stationery House
113 High Street
Cuckfield RH17 5JX
Tel: 01444 473355
Fax: 01444 473366
srg@splashdistribution.co.uk

FRANKE UK LTD
*Sinks in stainless steel, ceramic and
high-spec composites. Taps, work-
centre accessories and water
purification systems.*
West Park, Manchester International
Office Centre
Styal Road
Manchester M22 5BW
Tel: 0161 436 6280
Fax: 0161 436 2180
info.uk@franke.com
www.franke.co.uk

GEMINI BATH & KITCHEN
PRODUCTS
1501 E. Broadway
Tuscon AZ85719
USA

Tel: +1 520 770 0667
Fax: +1 520 770 9964
www.geminibkp.com

GROHE GMBH
*Kitchen and bathroom taps and
showers.*
Postfach 1353
32457 Porta Westfalica, Germany
Tel: +49 18 02/66 00 00
www.grohe.com
Available in the UK through:
Grohe Ltd
1 River Road
Barking IG11 0HD
Tel: 020 8594 7292
Fax: 020 8594 8898
info@grohe.co.uk
www.grohe.co.uk

HANSGROHE GMBH
*Axor, Pharo and Hansgrohe taps.
Also whirlpool baths, airbaths
and showers.*
Auestr. 5–9
77761 Schiltach, Germany
Tel: +49 7836 51 0
Fax: +49 7836 51 1300
www.hansgrohe.com
Available in the UK through:
Hansgrohe
Units D1 & D2
Sandown Trading Estate
Esher KT10 8BL
Tel: 01372 465655
Fax: 01372 470670
info@hansgrohe.co.uk
www.hansgrohe.co.uk

HARRINGTON BRASS
Tel: +1 201 818 1300
Fax: +1 201 818 0099
hwb@harringtonbrassworks.com

HERBEAU CREATIONS
*Period-style taps, brass and ceramic
sinks and bathroom fittings.*
177 Rue Anatole France
59790 Ronchin, France
Tel: +33 320 52 74 48
Fax: +33 320 52 25 73
herbeau@earthlink
Available in the UK through:
B.P. Wynn Co.
60 Queenstown Road
London SW8 3RY
Tel: 020 7498 4345
Fax: 020 7498 4346

SAMUEL HEATH AND SONS PLC
*Taps, showers, bathroom
accessories, architectural hardware.*
Leopold Street
Birmingham B12 0UJ
Tel: 0121 772 2303
Fax: 0121 772 3334
info@samuel-heath.com
www.samuel-heath.com

TONI ARMATUR
toni-armatur@post.tele.dk
www.toni.dk
Available in the UK through:
Thor Designs
Firside, Moneyrow Green
Holyport SL6 2 ND
Tel: 01628 634401

T & S BRASS AND BRONZE
WORKS INC.
Tel: +1 800 476 4103
Fax: +1 800 868 0084
www.tsbrass.com

VOLA
*Range of Arne Jacobsen
designed taps.*
Lunavej 2
DK-8700 Horsens, Denmark
Tel: +45 7023 5500
Fax: +45 7023 5511
sales@vola.dk
www.vola.co.uk
Available in the UK through:
Unit 12, Ampthill Business Park
Station Road
Ampthill MK45 2QW
Tel: 01525 841155
Fax: 01525 841177
sales@vola.co.uk
www.vola.co.uk

WATER REGULATORY ADVISORY
SERVICE (WRAS)
*Check with this body before
installing any fitting which does not
have approval for UK.*
Fern Close
Pen-y-fan Industrial Estate
Oakdale
Gwent NP11 3EH

appliances

AGA RAYBURN
Range cookers and stoves.
Station Road, Ketley
Telford TF1 5AQ
Tel: 01952 642000
Fax: 01952 222048
info@aga-rayburn.co.uk
www.aga-rayburn.co.uk

AMANA
www.amana.com
Available in the UK through:
Bradshaw Appliances
Kenn Road
Clevedon BS21 6LH
Tel: 01275 343000
Fax: 01275 343454
info@bradshaw.co.uk
www.bradshaw.co.uk

BOFFI
Kitchens and appliances.
Via Oberdan 70
20030 Lentate s/S(Mi), Italy

Tel: +39 0362 5341
Fax: +39 0362 565077
Available in the UK through:
Alternative Plans
(See Bathrooms)

BOSCH
*Built-in and freestanding appliances,
including dishwashers, home
laundry and refrigeration, hobs,
hoods and ovens.*
Grand Union House
Old Wolverton Road
Wolverton
Milton Keynes MK12 5PT
Tel: 08702 400060
Fax: 01908 328560
www.boschappliances.co.uk

BRITANNIA
The Range Cooker Co. plc.
Range House
281 Bristol Avenue
Blackpool FY2 0JF
Tel: 01253 471111
Fax: 01253 471136
enquiry@rangecooker.co.uk
www.rangecooker.co.uk

FISHER & PAYKEL APPLIANCES
*Laundry, refrigeration, dishwashing,
cooking appliances.*
Broxell Close
Wedgnock Industrial Estate
Warwick CV34 5QF
Tel: 01926 626 700
Fax: 01926 626 701
troy.scragg@fp.co.nz
www.fisherpaykel.com

FRIGIDAIRE
*Cookers, dishwashers, freezers,
refrigerators and laundry appliances.*
Electrolux International
3 Parkway Center
Pittsburgh PA 15220
USA
Tel: +1 412 928 8100
www.frigidaire.com

GAGGENAU HAUS GERATE GMBH
Domestic appliances.
Postfach 1201
D-76552 Gaggenau
Baden, Germany
Tel: +49 7225 78026
Fax: +49 7225 967190
www.gaggenau.com
Available in the UK through:
Gaggenau UK
Grand Union House
Old Wolverton Road
Old Wolverton
Milton Keynes MK12 5PT
Tel: 01908 328360
Fax: 01908 328370

GE (GENERAL ELECTRIC)
*Refrigerators and freezers, washers
and dryers, dishwashers,
compactors, cookers.*
Tel: +1 800 626 2000
www.geappliances.com
Available in the UK through:
GE Appliances UK Ltd
MBD Centre
Crompton Road
Stevenage SG1 2EE
Tel: 0800 731 8657
Fax: 0800 028 3420
geasalesuk@appl.ge.com

KITCHENAID
Counter-top and major appliances.
1701 KitchenAid Way
Greenville OH 45331
USA
Tel: +1 800 541 6390
Fax: +1 800 422 1230
www.kitchenaid.com

MIELE
www.miele.de
Available in the UK through:
Miele Company Limited
Fairacres, Marcham Road
Abingdon OX14 1TW
Tel: 01235 554455
Fax: 01235 554477
www.miele.co.uk

SMEG (UK) LTD
*Italian manufacturers of domestic
appliances.*
3 Park Square
Milton Park
Abingdon OX14 4RY
Tel: 0870 990 9907
www.smeguk.com

SUB-ZERO
Refrigeration.
Wolf Appliances Co. LLC
P.O. Box 44848,
Madison WI 53744
USA
Tel: +1 800 222 7820
Fax: +1 608 271 2233
www.subzero.com
Available in the UK through:
American Appliance Centre
Unit 5, The Dencora Centre
Dundee Way, Mollison Avenue
Enfield EN3 7SX
Tel: 020 8443 9999
Fax: 020 8443 9988
sales@american-appliance.co.uk
www.american-appliance.co.uk

VIKING
*Professional range cookers,
refrigeration, ovens and dishwashers.*
www.vikingrange.com
Available in the UK through:
Bradshaw Appliances

Kenn Road
Clevedon BS21 6LH
Tel: 01275 343000
Fax: 01275 343454
info@bradshaw.co.uk
www.bradshaw.co.uk

BATHROOMS

fittings & fixtures

AGAPE SRL
Via Po Barna 69
46031 Corregio Micheli di Bagnolo
San Vito (MN), Italy
Tel: +39 0376 250311
Fax: +39 0376 250330
info@agapedesign.it
www.agapedesign.it

ALTERNATIVE PLANS
*Stockists of contemporary Italian
Agape bathrooms and Boffi kitchens.*
9 Hester Road
London SW11 4AN
Tel: 020 7228 6460
Fax: 020 7924 1164
altplans@circon.co.uk
www.alternative-plans.co.uk

ARMITAGE SHANKS
*Wide range of bathroom suites, taps,
showers and accessories.*
Armitage, Rugeley
Staffs WS15 4BT
Tel: 01543 490253
Fax: 01543 491677
armitage-shanks@aseur.com
www.armitage-shanks.co.uk

ASSOCIATED METAL
(STAINLESS) LTD
*Produce Steristeel standard and
commercial stainless-steel fittings
and make to order.*
101 Brook Street
Glasgow G40 EAP
Tel: 0141 551 0707
Fax: 0141 551 0690
www.assoc-metal.co.uk

BARBER WILSONS & CO
Traditional taps and shower fittings.
(See Kitchens)

JEFF BELL CAST GLASS
*Made-to-order baths, basins and
shower screens.*
299 Haggerston Road
London E8 4EN
Tel: 020 7275 8481
www.glasscasts.co.uk

BISQUE
Designer radiators.
244 Belsize Road
London NW6 4BT
Tel: 020 7328 2225

Fax: 020 7328 9845
mail@bisque.co.uk
www.bisque.co.uk

BOWDEN GLASS LTD
*Specialize in bending glass for
lanterns, screens, shower cubicles,
as featured p160br.*
10 Marshgate Lane
Stratford
London E15 2NH
Tel: 020 8555 9660
Fax: 020 8519 5934

CLOAKROOM SOLUTIONS
*Basins in glass, silicone and
stainless steel, taps and cloakroom
accessories. Suppliers of the Pollux
series basin.*
Unit 8, The Courtyard
Holmbush Farm
Faygate RH12 4SE
Tel: 0700 2345 111
Fax: 0700 2345 222
www.cloakroomsolutions.co.uk

COLOURWASH
*Well-edited selection of
contemporary bathroom fittings
and accessories.*
165 Chamberlayne Road
London NW10 3NU
Tel: 020 8459 8918
Fax: 020 8459 4280
sales@colourwash.co.uk
www.colourwash.co.uk

C.P. HART
*Bathroom ceramics, furniture, taps,
baths, showers and accessories.*
Newnham Terrace
Hercules Road
London SE1 7DR
Tel: 020 7902 1000
Fax: 020 7902 1001
www.cphart.co.uk

DORNBRACHT
(See Kitchens)

DÜKER SANITÄR GMBH
Am Wendelsberg 24
97289 Thüngen, Germany
Tel: + 49 9360/90620
Fax: +49 9360/906239
info@dueker-sanitaer.de
www.dueker-sanitaer.de
Available from C.P. Hart (see above)

DURAVIT AG
Werderstrasse 36
D-7832 Hornberg, Germany
Tel: +49 78 33 70 0
Fax: +49 78 33 70 289
info@duravit.de
www.duravit.com
Available from C.P. Hart (see above)

GEC ANDERSON
Stainless-steel sinks, bowls, baths, WCs and worktops for domestic and commercial use.
(See Kitchens)

GROHE
Traditional and contemporary taps and showers.
(See Kitchens)

HANSGROHE
Showerheads and taps in contemporary designs.
(See Kitchens)

HARRIS FABRICATIONS
Made-to-order stainless-steel bathroom fittings. Producers of custom-made shower base featured p160br.
Unit 7, Billet Works
Billet Road
London E17 5DT
Tel: 0208 531 7024
harrisfab@dial.pipex.com
www.harrisfabrication.co.uk

JACUZZI
Sanitaryware, showers, brassware, whirlpool baths and accessories.
Silverdale Road
Newcastle under Lyme ST5 6EL
Tel: 01782 717175
Fax: 01782 717166
helenbray@jacuzziuk.com
www.jacuzzi.co.uk

KOHLER
Bathroom fittings, taps and showers.
444 Highland Drive
Kohler WI 53044
USA
Tel: +1 920 457 4441
www.kohler.com

PERRIN & ROWE
Traditional-style taps and shower fittings, including the Country set, similar to that featured p167c.
Avilion Ltd
Orwell Close
Fairview Industrial Park
Manor Way
Rainham RM13 8UB
Tel: 01708 526361
Fax: 01708 550220
sales@avilion.co.uk
www.avilion.co.uk

SAMUEL HEATH & SONS PLC
Taps, showers, bathroom accessories, architectural hardware.
(See Kitchens)

B.C. SANITAN
Traditional-style bathroom fittings.
(See Jacuzzi)

SANTRIC LTD
Stainless-steel lavatories, industrial sinks and basins.
Downley Road
Havant PO9 2YD
Tel: 023 9248 8755
Fax: 023 9248 8766
info@santric.co.uk
www.santric.co.uk

SOTTINI
Bathroom fittings and taps.
The Bathroom Works
National Avenue
Kingston upon Hull HU5 4HS
Tel: 01482 449513
Fax: 01482 445886
www.sottini.co.uk

VOLA
Taps.
(See Kitchens)

W & G SISSONS
Sinks, taps and lavatories designed for commercial premises in stainless steel.
Carrwood Road
Sheepbridge
Chesterfield S41 9QB
Tel: 01246 450255
Fax: 01246 451276
wgs@sissons.co.uk
www.sissons.co.uk

PHILIP WISH
Interior designer and concrete designer/maker.
38 Stradella Road
London SE24 9HA
Tel: 020 7737 7797

LINEABETA
Bathroom accessories.
Strada Statale 11
KM331-36053 Gambellara V1
Italy
Tel: +39 444 644 644
Fax: +39 444 644 600
www.lineabeta.com

surface finishes
EDGAR UDNY
Mosaic and swimming-pool tiles, featured p172c.
(See Kitchens)

FIRED EARTH
Wall and floor tiles and bathroom fittings.
(See Flooring)

HARVEY MARIA
Cork tiles printed with photographic images.
Trident Business Centre
89 Bickersteth Road

London SW17 9SH
Tel: 020 8516 7788
Fax: 020 8516 7789
www.harveymaria.co.uk

LIMESTONE GALLERY
Limestone tiles and slabs. Bespoke limestone for kitchen worktops, bathrooms, fire surrounds, etc.
Arch 47, South Lambeth Road
London SW8 1SS
Tel: 020 7735 8555
Fax: 020 7793 8880
limestoneg@aol.com
www.limestonegallery.co.uk

LITHOFIN
German range of sealing, cleaning and protection products.
www.lithofin.de
Available in the UK through:
Casdron
Wood End
Prospect Road
Alresford SO24 9QF
Tel: 01962 732126
Fax: 01962 735373
sales@lithofin.co.uk
www.lithofin.co.uk

LONGMEAD CERAMICS
Ceramic tiles including tiles with integral bathroom accessories.
Millway Industrial Estate
Axminster EX3 5HU
Tel: 01297 32578

LUXCRETE
Glass blocks for domestic and commercial use. Products featured p61ar and p161br.
(See Walls & Ceilings)

MAJESTIC SHOWER COMPANY LTD
Shower doors, enclosures and bath screens.
1 North Place
Edinburgh Way
Harlow CM20 2SL
Tel: 01279 443644
Fax: 01279 635074
info@majesticshowers.com
www.majesticshowers.com

PERSPEX
Perspex, Prismex and Lucite acrylic sheet. A list of fabricators can be found on the websites.
Tel: 01254 874000
www.perspex.co.uk
www.lucite.com

TIKKURILA COATINGS LTD
Speacialist coatings including chlorinated rubber paint for swimming pools.
Warth Mills
Radcliffe Road

Bury BL9 9NB
Tel: 0161 764 6017
info@tikkurila.co.uk
www.tikkurila-coatings.co.uk

ANTIQUES AND ARCHITECTURAL SALVAGE

THE ANTIQUE TRADER AT MILLINERY WORKS
Dealer in Arts and Crafts furniture and fittings.
85–87 Southgate Road
London N1 3JS
Tel: 020 7359 2019
Fax: 020 7359 5792
art@millineryworks.co.uk
www.millineryworks.co.uk

THE ARTS AND CRAFTS FURNITURE COMPANY
Original furniture, lighting, ceramics, fabrics, carpets and pictures.
49 Sheen Lane
London SW14 8AB
Tel: 020 8876 6544
www.artsandcraftsfurnitureco.co.uk

BAILEYS
The Engine Shed
Ashburton Ind. Estate
Ross-On-Wye HR9 7BW
Tel: 01989 563015
Fax: 01989 768172

BROOK HOUSE FARM
Salters Bridge
Tarvin Sands
Chester CH3 8NR
Tel: 01829 740883
Fax: 01829 740481

EASY
Fireplaces, bathroom fittings, radiators, doors and door furniture.
Unit 6, Couper Street
Edinburgh Way
Edinburgh EH6 6HH
Tel: 0131 554 7077
Fax: 0131 554 3070
www.easy-arch-salv.co.uk

THE HOUSE HOSPITAL
Architectural salvage, including doors, fireplaces, radiators, baths, basins and taps.
9 Ferrier Street
London SW18 1SW
Tel: 020 8870 8202
info@thehousehospital.com
www.thehousehospital.com

LASSCO
Cast-iron radiators, bathroom fittings, butler's sinks and taps.
41 Maltby Street
London SE1 3PA

Tel: 020 7394 7788
Fax: 020 7327 8373
rbk@lassco.co.uk
www.lassco.co.uk

OLLIFF'S ARCHITECTURAL ANTIQUES
Fireplaces, timber flooring and tiles, doors and door furniture, panelling, radiators and bathroomware.
21 Lower Redland Rd
Bristol BS6 6TB
Tel: 0117 923 9232
Fax: 0117 923 9880
marcus@olliffs.com
www.olliffs.com

POSTERITY
Fireplaces, doors, sanitaryware, brassware, radiators, lighting, stained-glass panels, and flooring.
Underhill Farm
Little Malvern WR14 4JN
Tel: 01684 541254
Fax: 01684 541256

RIBBLE RECLAMATION
The Brick House
Ducie Place
Preston PR1 4UJ
Tel: 01772 794534
Fax: 01772 794604

RONSON'S RECLAMATION
Stone flooring, bricks and roof tiles, timbers, baths and kitchen sinks. Also bespoke stone fireplaces.
Norton Barns Comples
Wainlodes Lane
Norton GL2 9LN
Tel: 01452 731236
Fax: 01452 731888
www.ronsonreclamation.com

SOLOPARK
Good for building materials and reclaimed wood flooring.
(See Wooden Flooring)

WALCOT RECLAMATION
Architectural antiques, including fireplaces, doors and radiators.
108 Walcot Street
Bath BA1 5BG
Tel: 01225 444404
Fax: 01225 448163
rick@walcot.com
www.walcot.com

WALCOT RECLAMATION DEPOT
Reclaimed floorboards, parquet, flagstones and quarry tiles.
Riverside Business Park
Lower Bristol Road
Bath BA2 3DW
Tel: 01225 335532
Fax: 01225 484317
www.walcot.com

ARCHITECTS AND DESIGNERS WHOSE WORK IS FEATURED IN THIS BOOK

JONATHAN ADLER
465 Broome Street
New York NY 10013
USA
Tel: +1 212 941 8950
Pottery lighting and textiles
Page 102b.

ANDERSON ARCHITECTS
555 West 25th Street
New York NY 10001
USA
Tel: +1 212 620 0996
Fax: +1 212 620 5299
info@andersonarch.com
www.andersonarch.com
Page 67bl.

NICHOLAS ARBUTHNOTT
Arbuthnott Ladenbury Architects
Architects & Urban Designers
15 Gosditch Street
Cirencester GL7 2AG
and
VANESSA ARBUTHNOTT FABRICS
The Tallet
Calmsden
Cirencester GL7 5ET
www.vanessaarbuthnott.co.uk
and
COUNTRY HOUSE WALKS LTD
Self-catering accommodation/
weekend breaks
The Tallet
Calmsden
Cirencester GL7 5ET
www.thetallet.co.uk
Pages 15r, 154al.

ASFOUR GUZY
594 Broadway, Suite 1204
New York NY 10012
USA
Tel: +1 212 334 9350
Fax: +1 212 334 9009
Page 122br.

ASH SAKULA ARCHITECTS
24 Rosebery Avenue
London EC1R 4SX
Tel: 020 7837 9735
Fax: 020 7837 9708
robert@ashsak.com
www.ashsak.com
Pages 55br, 129br,146al, 149br,
154ac, 155ac.

AZMAN OWENS
Architects
8 St Albans place
London NW1 0NX
Tel: 020 7354 2955
Fax: 020 7354 2966
Pages 50al, 158al.

BABYLON DESIGN LTD
Lighting Designers
301 Fulham Road
London SW10 9QH
Tel: 020 7376 7233
info@babylondesign.demon.co.uk
Lights by up-and-coming designers
such as Peter Wylly, Ross Menuez
and Roland Simmons
Page 132a.

JOHN BARMAN INC.
Interior design & decoration
500 Park Avenue
New York NY 10022
USA
Tel: +1 212 838 9443
john@barman.com
www.johnbarman.com
Pages 8a, 19al, 136, 145bl, 150a,
150bl, 150bc, 152a, 157al, 165ar.

BATAILLE & iBENS
Claire Bataille & Paul ibens
Design NV
Architects
Vekestratt 13 Bus 14
2000 Antwerpen
Belgium
Tel: +32 3 231 3593
Fax: +32 3 213 8639
Pages 57r, 60bl, 86ar, 86br, 99a,
106br, 172bc.

CHARLES BATESON DESIGN
CONSULTANTS
Interior Design
18 Kings Road
St Margaret's
Twickenham TW1 2QS
Tel: 020 8892 3141
Fax: 020 8891 6483
Charles.bateson@btinternet.com
Pages 3c, 3r, 6ac, 9br, 19bl, 21c,
29br, 36ar, 55ar, 90, 100ar, 108a,
142bc, 158br, 166ac, 168ar.

ROBERTO BERGERO
Interior Designer
4 rue St. Gilles
75003 Paris
France
Tel: +33 1 42 72 03 51
robertobergero@club-internet.fr
Page 70b.

BILHUBER INC
330 East 59th Street, 6th Floor
New York NY 10022
USA
Tel: +1 212 308 4888
Pages 73al, 103ar.

STEPHEN BLATT ARCHITECTS
Architectural Design Firm
10, Danforth Street
Portland, Maine 04101
USA
Tel: +1 207 761 5911
Fax: +1 207 761 2105
sba@sbarchitects.com
Page 103al.

L.B.D.A.
Laura Bohn Design Associates, Inc.
30 West 26th Street
New York NY 10010
USA
Tel: +1 212 645 3636
Fax: +1 212 645 3639
Pages 120cr, 122bl.

FELIX BONNIER
7 rue St Claude
75003 Paris
France
Tel: +33 42 26 09 83
Pages 36al, 146bl.

BOWLES & LINARES
32 Hereford Road
London W2 5AJ
Tel: 020 7229 9886
Pages 9bl, 20al, 139cr.

BRIFFA PHILIPS
19–21 Holywell Hill
St Albans
Herts AL1 1EZ
Tel: 01727 840567
Page 64bl.

MARK BROOK DESIGN
7 Sunderland Terrace
London W2 5PA
Tel: 020 7221 8106
Pages 153bl, 154ar.

BROOKES STACEY RANDALL
New Hibernia House
Winchester Walk
London SE1 9AG
Tel: 020 7403 0707
Fax: 020 7403 0880
info@bsr-architects.com
Pages 9bc, 30c, 31, 58–59, 100al,
162ac.

HUGH BROUGHTON ARCHITECTS
Award winning architects
4 Addison Bridge Place
London W14 8XP
Tel: 020 7602 8840
Fax: 020 7602 5254
hugh@hbarchitects.demon.co.uk
Pages 2bl, 50ar, 137br, 145al.

CABOT DESIGN LTD
Interior Design
1925 Seventh Avenue, Suite 71
New York NY10026
USA
Tel: +1 212 222 9488
eocabot@aol.com
Page 97

CARDEN CUNIETTI
83 Westbourne Park Road
London W2 5QH
Tel: 020 7229 8559
Fax: 020 7229 8799
www.carden-cunietti.com
Pages 168br, 169br.

GARTH CARTER
Specialist interiors painter
Tel: 0958 412953
Page 164l.

CIRCUS ARCHITECTS
Unit 1, Summer Street
London EC1R 5BD
Tel: 020 7833 1999
Pages 50b, 53bl, 57l, 60al, 60cl,
61ar, 64br, 65, 78l, 119a, 122al,
129ar, 152bl.

DAVID COLLINS
Architecture & Design
Unit 6 & 7
Chelsea Wharf
Lots Road
London SW10 0QJ
Tel: 020 7349 5900
Page 20br.

SIMON CONDER ASSOCIATES
Architects & Designers
Nile Street Studios
8 Nile street
London N1 7RF
Tel: 020 7251 2144
Fax: 020 7251 2145
e.simon@simonconder.co.uk
Pages 161bl, 164r.

DLB CORDIER
Church Farm Oast Conversion by DLB
Cordier-*Architect*
danielcordier@compuserve.com
Pages 67al, 85cr, 99b.

DAD ASSOCIATES
112–6 Old Street
London EC1V 9BD
Tel: 020 7336 6488
Pages 42b, 172c.

JOËLLE DARBY
Architect
Darby Maclellan Partnership
Unit 3 Limehouse Cut
46 Morris Road
London E14 6NQ
Tel: 020 7987 4432
darby.maclellan@tinyonline.co.uk
Page 160cl.

SANDY DAVIDSON DESIGN
1505 Viewsite Terrace
Los Angeles, CA 90069
USA
Fax: +1 320 659 2107
SandSandD@aol.com
Pages 26a, 78r, 161a.

DOLS WONG ARCHITECTS
Architects specialising in private
residences, one-off shops and
restaurants.
Loft 3, 329 Harrow Road
London W9 3RB
Tel: 020 7266 2129
Fax: 020 7266 2179
dolswong@btinternet.com
Pages 1, 2cr, 6br, 19br, 91al, 111br,
113br, 120ac, 120br, 121.

ROBERT DYE ASSOCIATES
68–74 Rochester Place
London NW1 9JX
Page 42ar.

EGER ARCHITECTS
Architects & Landscape Architects
2 D'eynsford Road
London SE5 7EB
Tel: 020 7701 6771
Fax: 020 7708 5716
design@egerarchitects.com
www.egerarchitects.com
Pages 5, 9ar, 11al, 19ac, 19ar, 20c,
24al, 28al, 28ac, 30ar, 45al, 98b,
122bc.

EMERY & CIE AND NOIR D'IVORIE
Rue de L'Hôpital 25–29
Brussels
Belgium
Tel: +32 2 513 5892
Fax: +32 5 513 3970
Pages 33r, 39ar.

FAT
Appletree Cottage
116–120 Golden Lane
London EC1Y 0TL
Tel: 020 7251 6735
Fax: 020 7251 6730
fat@fat.co.uk
www.fat.co.uk
Page 15c.

FILER & COX
Architectural Deviants
194 Bermondsey Street
London SE1 3TQ
Tel: 020 7357 7574
Fax: 020 7357 7573
iru@filerandcox.com
www.filerandcox.com
Pages 7c, 20cl, 44, 72al, 72bl,
73bl, 142cr, 154bl, 157ac, 162br,
170b, 172bl.

GABELLINI ASSOCIATES
*Michael Gabellini AIA, Principal
designer. Dan Garbowit AIA,
Managing Principal Ralph Bellandi.
Sal Tranchina, Jonathan Knowles
AIA, Project Architects. Stephanie
Kim, Lisa Monteleone, Tom
Vandenbout, Project Team.*
665 Broadway, Suite 706
New York NY 10012
USA
Tel: +1 212 388 1700
Fax: +1 212 388 1808
Page 61c.

ZINA GLAZEBROOK
ZG Design
10 Wireless Road
East Hampton NY 11937
USA
Tel: +1 631 329 7486
Fax: +1 631 329 2087
dzina@ATT.net
www.zgdesign.com
Pages 34–35.

GLOSS LTD
Designers of home accessories
274 Portobello Road
London W10 5TE
Tel: 020 8960 4146
Fax: 020 8960 4842
pascale@glossltd.u-net.com
Pages 96–97.

CHRISTOPHE GOLLUT
Alistair Covlin Limited
116 Fulham Road
London SW3 6HU
Pages 38–39, 39b.

JAMES GORST ARCHITECTS
35 Lambs Conduit Street
London WC1N 3NG
Tel: 020 7831 8300
Pages 66a, 66cr, 91ar, 158bl.

HESTER GRAY
25 Pembridge Villas
London W11 3EP
Tel: 020 7229 3162
Page 155b.

MARK GUARD ARCHITECTS
161 Whitfield Street
London W1P 5RY
Tel: 020 7380 1199
Pages 29ar, 43a.

WILLIAM R. HEFNER AIA
William Hefner Architect L.L.C
5820 Wilshire Boulevard, Suite 601
Los Angeles CA 90036
USA
Tel: +1 323 931 1365
Fax: +1 323 931 1368
wh@williamhefner.com
www.williamhefner.com
Pages 26a, 78r, 161a.

ALASTAIR HENDY
*Food writer, art director and
designer*
Fax: 020 7739 6040
Pages 58, 101b, 169ac.

GUY HILLS
Photographer
Tel/fax: 020 7916 2610
guyhills@hotmail.com
Pages 7a, 22, 28ar, 35c&bl, 59, 81r,
98ac.

HIRST PACIFIC LTD
250 Lafayette Street
New York NY 10012
USA
Tel: +1 212 625 3670
Fax: +1 212 625 3673
hirstpacific@earthlink.net
Pages 62–63, 139c.

HM2 ARCHITECTS
*Architects & Designers
Richard Webb, Project Director
Andrew Hanson, Director*
33–37 Charterhouse Square
London EC1M 6EA
Tel: 020 7600 5151
Fax: 020 7600 1092
andrew.hanson@harper-mackay.co.uk
Pages 17, 166cl.

PHILIP HOOPER
Interior Designer
Studio 30
The Old Latchmere School
38 Burns Road
London SW11 5GY
Tel: 020 7978 6662
Fax: 020 7223 3713
Page 103bl.

JOHN C HOPE
Architects
3 St. Bernard's Crescent
Edinburgh EH4 1NR
Tel: 0131 315 2215
Fax: 0131 315 2911
Pages 25b, 42al, 85br.

HUDSON FEATHERSTONE
ARCHITECTS
49–59 Old Street
London EC1V 9HX
Tel: 020 7490 5656
Pages 34c, 45b, 53al, 82a, 87.

HUT SACHS STUDIO
Architecture & Interior Design
414 Broadway
New York NY 10013
USA
Tel: +1 212 219 1567
Fax: +1 212 219 1677
hutsachs@hutsachs.com
www.hutsachs.com
Page 142a.

INTERNI PTY LTD
Interior Design Consultancy
15–19 Boundary Street
Rushcutter's Bay
Sydney 2010
Australia
Pages 7b, 12, 39br.

MALIN IOVINO DESIGN
Tel: 020 7252 3542
Fax: 020 7252 3542
iovino@btinternet.com
Pages 125ar, 125ac.

IPL INTERIORS
Thames House, Unit 26Cl
140 Battersea Park Road
London SW11 4NY
Tel: 020 7622 3009
Fax: 020 7622 2246
ipl.interiors@virgin.net
Pages 14bc, 38bl, 71 all above, 89al,
91br, 95, 100b, 108bl, 111a both,
111cl, 117r, 118al, 123bl, 126al,
135ar, 135bc.

GAVIN JACKSON
Tel: 07050 097561
Page 139bl.

JOANNA JEFFERSON ARCHITECTS
222 Oving Road
Chichester PO19 4EJ
Tel: 01243 532398
Fax: 01243 531 550
jjeffearch@aol.com
Page 67br.

JOHNSON NAYLOR
13 Britton Street
London EC1M 5SX
Tel: 020 7490 8885
Fax: 020 7490 0038
brian.johnson@johnsonnaylor.co.uk
Pages 56, 66cl, 172ac.

JUAN PECK FOON
*Resources + Planning Design
Consultants*
73 Cardiff Grove
Singapore 558939
Tel: +65 382 4518
Fax: +65 382 4865
peckfoon@singnet.com.sg
Page 30bl.

JUST DESIGN LTD
80 Fifth Avenue, 18th Floor
New York NY 10011
USA
Tel: +1 212 243 6544
Fax: +1 212 229 1112
wbp@angel.net
Page 13.

ANGELA KEARSEY DESIGNS
*General interior design and
decoration – wall/floor coverings,
curtains, fabrics and accessories.*
Tel: 020 7483 0967
Fax: 020 7483 1629
Angela.Kearsey@btinternet.com
Pages 1, 2cr, 6br, 19br, 91al, 111br,
113br, 120ac, 120br, 121.

SEAN KELLY GALLERY
528 West 29th Street
New York NY 10001
USA
Tel: +1 212 239 1181
Fax: +1 212 239 2467
www.skny.com
Pages 14bl, 113al, 141bl.

ANGELA KENT
Architect
Kenström Design Pty Ltd
92 Cathedral Street
Woolloomooloo NSW 2011
Australia
Page 139br.

STEVEN LEARNER STUDIO
Architecture and interior design
307 Seventh Avenue
New York NY 10001
USA
Tel: +1 212 741 8583
Fax: +1 212 741 2180
info@stevenlearnerstudio.com
www.stevenlearnerstudio.com
Pages 14bl, 113al, 141bl.

KAYODE LIPEDE
Tel: 020 7794 7535
Page 152bl.

DALE LOTH ARCHITECTS
1 Cliff Road
London NW1 9AJ
Tel: 020 7485 4003
Fax: 020 7284 4490
mail@dalelotharchitects.ltd.uk
Pages 165bl, 165bc, 169cr.

RANDALL L. MAKINSON
RLM Associates
Restoration Consultants
Fax: +1 626 449 2059
makinson@earthlink.net
Page 120cl.

NICOLETTA MARAZZA
Via G Morone, 8
20121 Milan
Italy
Tel/fax: +39 2 7601 4482
Pages 105bl, 115al.

MARINO + GIOLITO
161 West 16th Street
New York NY 10011
USA
Tel/fax: +1 212 675 5737
Pages 113ar, 166al, 170c.

MARMOL & RADZINER +
ASSOCIATES, ARCHITECTURE +
CONSTRUCTION
2902, Nebraska Avenue
Santa Monica CA 90404
USA
Tel: +1 310 264 1814
Fax: +1 310 264 1817
www.marmol-radziner.com
Pages 26–27a, 81l.

PAUL MATHIEU
Interior Design
France:
12 rue Matheron
13100 Aix-en-Provence
France
Tel: +33 4 42 23 97 77
Fax: +33 4 42 23 97 59
USA:
7 East 14th Street, # 805
New York NY 10003
USA
Tel: +1 646 638 4531
Page 171al.

MCDOWELL + BENEDETTI
62 Rosebury Avenue
London EC1R 4RR
Tel: 020 7278 8810
Pages 37a, 41a.

DAVID MELLOR DESIGN
David Mellor cutlery is manufactured in the Round Building; the Country Shop sells cutlery, kitchenware, tableware and British craftware.
The Round Building & Country Shop
Hathersage
Sheffield S32 1BA
Tel: 01433 650220
Fax: 01433 650944
davidmellor@UKOnline.co.uk
Page 62r.

JEAN-LOUIS MÉNARD
32 Boulevard de l'Hopital
75005 Paris
France
Tel: +33 43 36 31 74
Page 165al.

FRÉDÉRIC MÉRCHICHE
4 rue de Thorigny
75003 Paris
France
Pages 33bl, 45ac.

DAVID MIKHAIL ARCHITECTS
68/74 Rochester Place
London NW1 9JX
Tel: 020 7485 4696
Fax: 020 7267 8661
www.dmikhail.freeserve.co.uk
Pages 165br, 170al.

MONEO BROCK STUDIO
371 Broadway
New York NY 10013
USA
Tel: +1 212 625 0308
Fax: +1 212 625 0309
www.moneobrock.com
Pages 2al, 6al, 18al, 18r, 88, 93ar, 140cr, 142a, 147a, 151al, 151ac, 153cl, 154–155b 155c, 160a, 167a.

MOOArc
Architects
198 Blackstock Road
London N5 1EN
Tel: 020 7354 1729
Fax: 020 7354 1730
studio@mooarc.com
www.mooarc.com
Pages 29al, 86l, 91bc.

MOORE RUBLE YUDELL ARCHITECTS & PLANNERS.
933 Pico Boulevard
Santa Monica CA 90405
USA
Tel: +1 310 450 1400
Fax: +1 310 450 1403
Pages 11bl, 24c.

MULLMAN SEIDMAN ARCHITECTS
Architecture & interior design
443 Greenwich Street, # 2A
New York NY 10013
USA
Tel: +1 212 431 0770
Fax: +1 212 431 8428
msa@mullmanseidman.com
dmullman@mullmanseidman.com
pseidman@mullmanseidman.com
www.mullmanseidman.com
Pages 8c, 8b,20ac, 89bl, 98ar, 105al, 106bl, 112, 124r, 127l, 135br, 137ar, 140br, 141al, 143a, 143b, 148r, 152br, 153br, 157b, 171ar, 171b, 173l.

FRANÇOIS MURACCIOLE
Architect
54 rue de Montreuil
75011 Paris
France
Tel: +33 1 43 71 33 03
francois.muracciole@libertysurf.fr
Pages 71c, 117l, 133al.

MUSEUM OF WELSH LIFE
St Fagan's
Cardiff CF5 6XB
Wales
Page 68b.

MICHAEL NATHENSON
Unique Environments
Design & Architecture
33 Florence Street
London N1 2FW
Tel: 020 7431 6978
Fax: 020 7431 6975
mbn@compuserve.com
www.unique-environments.co.uk
Pages 2ar, 2cl, 19cl, 20al, 20cr, 89c, 89r, 92, 93al, 104, 105br, 108c, 108br, 109, 110a both, 110br, 137al, 137bl, 141r, 149l, 153ar, 162al, 171ac, 172ar.

ROGER OATES DESIGN
Rugs and runners
Shop & Showroom:
1 Munro Terrace
off Cheyne Walk
Chelsea
London SW10 0DL
Studio Shop:
The Long Barn
Eastnor
Ledbury
Herefordshire HR8 1EL
Mail Order Catalogue:
Tel: 01531 631611
Pages 53br, 54cr.

OGAWA/DEPARDON ARCHITECTS
137 Varick Street, 4th floor
New York NY 10013
USA
Tel: +1 212 627 7390
Fax: +1 212 627 9681
ogawdep@aol.com
Pages 27, 76a, 79.

OREFELT ASSOCIATES
Design Team: Gunner Orefelt, John Massey, Gianni Botsford, Jason Griffiths
4 Portobello Studios
5 Haydens Place
London W11 1LY
Tel: 020 7243 3181
Fax: 020 7792 1126
orefelt@msn.com
Pages 9cr, 139al, 156, 161br, 162bl, 170ar.

PARNASSUS
Corso Porta Vittoria, 5
Milan
Italy
Tel: +39 02 78 11 07
Page 147c

CAROLINE PATERSON
50 Lavender Gardens
London SW11 1DD
Page 158ar.

GRAHAM PHILLIPS
Pages 26–27b, 118–119.

CAMPION A PLATT
641 Fifth Avenue
New York NY 10022
USA
Page 35al.

JENNIFER POST DESIGN
Spatial & Interior Designer
25 East 67th Street, 8D
New York NY 10021
USA
Tel: +1 212 734 7994
Fax: +1 212 396 2450
jpostdesign@aol.com
Pages 24ac, 49r, 125br.

ALAN POWER ARCHITECTS
5 Haydens Place
London W11 1LY
Tel: 020 7229 9375
Fax: 020 7221 4172
Pages 75l, 76b, 83.

LENA PROUDLOCK
Denim in Style
Drews House
Leighterton
Gloucestershire GL8 8UN
Tel/fax: 01666 890230
Page 148al.

MARK PYNN A.I.A
McMillen Pynn Architecture LLP
PO Box 1068
Sun Valley ID 83353
USA
Tel: +1 208 622 4656
Fax: +1 208 726 7108
mpynn@sunvally.net
www.sunvalleyachitect.com
Pages 14br, 57c, 64al, 67ar.

KARIM RASHID INC.
Industrial design
357 W. 17th Street
New York NY 10011
USA
Tel: +1 212 929 8657
Fax: +1 212 929 0247
www.karimrashid.com
Pages 51, 137c, 145ar, 151b.

REED CREATIVE SERVICES LTD
151a Sydney Street
London SW3 6NT
Tel: 020 7565 0066
Pages 30al, 119b, 129bc.

NICO RENSCH ARCHITEAM
Tel: 0411 412 898
Pages 123br, 128, 131a.

RETROUVIUS
Architectural reclamation and design
Office:
32 York House
Upper Montagu Street
London W1H 1FR
Tel: 020 7724 3387
Warehouse/studio:
2A Ravensworth Road
London NW10 5NR
Tel: 020 8960 6060
mail@retrouvius.com
www.retrouvious.com
Pages 7a, 22, 28ar, 35l, 59, 81r, 98ac.

RHODE DESIGN
86 Stoke Newington Church Street
London N16 0AP
Tel: 020 7275 8261
Pages 21a, 142cl.

JOHANNE RISS
Stylist, designer and fashion designer.
35 Place du Nouveau Marché aux Graens
1000 Brussels
Belguim
Tel: +32 2 513 0900
Fax: +32 2 514 3284
Page 14al.

DAMIEN ROLAND
Architect
Agence du Centre
6, rue Clovis
45100 Orléans
France
Pages 24ar, 40.

PETER ROMANIUK
The Flower House
Cynthia Street
London N1 9JF
Tel: 020 7837 7373
Pages 20bc, 105ar, 110bl, 139bc.

LUIGI ROSSELLI
Surry Hills
2010 Sydney
New South Wales
Australia
Tel: +61 2 9281 1498
Pages 36bl.

EVELYNE ROUSSEL
Tel: +33 1 43 55 76 97
Page 98al.

CHARLES RUTHERFOORD
51 The Chase
London SW4 0NP
Pages 12–13, 41c, 46all above, 52ar, 158cl.

JOSEPHINE RYAN ANTIQUES
63 Abbeville Road
London SW4 9JW
Tel: 020 8675 3900
Pages 66b.

SAGE WIMER COOMBE ARCHITECTS
Project Team: Jennifer Sage, Peter Coombe, Suzan Selcuk, Peggy Tan.
480 Canal Street Room 1002
New York NY 10013
USA
Tel: +1 212 226 9600
Page 115ac.

SOPHIE SARIN
Tel: 020 7221 4635
Pages 20bl, 146bc.

SCDA ARCHITECTS
10 Teck Lim Road
Singapore 088386
Tel: +65 324 5458
Fax: +65 324 5450
scda@cyberway.com.sg
Pages 15l, 172al.

SCHEFER DESIGN
David Schefer & Eve-Lynn Schoenstein
41 Union Square West, No. 1427
New York NY 10003
Tel: +1 212 691 9097
Fax: +1 212 691 9520
scheferdesign@mindspring.com
www.scheferdesign.com
Page 102b.

SHEILA SCHOLES
Designer
Tel: 01480 498241
Pages 94a, 155ar.

JOHNSON SCHWINGHAMMER
339 West 38th Street # 9
New York NY 10018
USA
Tel: +1 212 643 1552
Pages 75br, 77, 85ac, 116, 130bl.

STEVEN SCLAROFF, DESIGNER
801 Greenwich Street
New York NY 10014
USA
Tel: +1 212 691 7814
Fax: +1 212 691 7793
sclaroff@aol.com
Pages 151ar, 155al.

MACK SCOGIN MERRILL ELAM
ARCHITECTS
Principal architects: Mack Scogin and Merrill Elam
75, J.W. Dobbs Avenue, N.E.
Atlanta, Georgia 30303
USA
Tel: +1 404 525 6869
Fax: +1 404 525 7061
Pages 25c, 64ar.

SERGISSION BATES
44 Newman Street
London W1P 3PA
Tel: 020 7255 1564
Fax: 020 7636 5646
Pages 101ar, 120al.

SHELTON, MINDEL & ASSOCIATES
216 West 18th Street
New York NY 10011
USA
Tel: +1 212 243 3939
Pages 75br, 77, 85ac, 116, 130bl.

SHEPPARD DAY DESIGN
Tel: 020 7821 2002
Pages 23, 91bl, 161bc.

KEN SHUTTLEWORTH
Architect
Page 25a.

SIDNAM PETRONE GARTNER
ARCHITECTS
Coty Sidnam, Bill Petrone and Eric Gartner
136 West 21st Street
New York NY 10011
USA
Tel: +1 212 366 5500
Fax: +1 212 366 6559
sidnampetr@aol.com
www.spgarchitects.com
Pages 24b, 166c.

STEPHEN SLAN A.I.A
Variations In Architecture Inc.
2156 Hollyridge Drive
Los Angeles CA 90068
USA
Tel: +1 323 467 4455
Fax: +1 323 467 6655
Pages 64bc, 68–69, 172br.

NIGEL SMITH
Architect
Tel: 020 7278 8802
n-smith@dircon.co.uk
Page 166cr.

SQUARE FOOT PROPERTIES LTD.
50 Britton Street
London EC1M 5UP
Tel: 020 7253 2527
Fax: 020 7253 2528
Page 85c.

GUY STANSFELD
Tel: 020 7727 0133
Pages 111bl, 114.

SETH STEIN ARCHITECT
15 Grand Union Centre
West Row
Ladbrooke Grove
London W10
Tel: 020 8968 8581
Pages 60bl, 61bl, 61br, 118bl, 120bl, 123a, 160bl, 162cr, 167b, 167al.

JOHN L. STEWART
SIT, L.L.C.
113–115 Bank Street
New York NY 10014
USA
Tel: +1 212 620 777
Fax: +1 212 620 0770
JLSCollection@aol.com
Page 71bl.

STICKLAND COOMBE
ARCHITECTURE
258 Lavender Hill
London SW11 1LJ
Tel: 020 7924 1699
Fax: 020 7652 1788
nick@scadesign.freserve.co.uk
Pages 173c.

SALLY STOREY
John Cullen Lighting
585 King's Road
London SW6 2EH
Tel: 020 7371 5400
Page 119b.

TONY SUTTLE
Woods Bagot Pty Ltd
Architects
64 Marine Parade
Southport
Queensland 4215
Australia
Page 16bl.

BRUNO TANQUEREL
Artist
2 Passage St. Sébastien
75011 Paris
France
Tel: +33 1 43 57 03 93
Pages 160bc, 166bc, 166br, 169al.

TAYLOR WOODROW CAPITAL
DEVELOPMENTS LTD.
International House
1 St Katherine's Way
London E1 9TW
Tel: 020 7488 0555
Page 20br.

TODHUNTER EARLE INTERIORS
Chelsea Reach, 1st floor
79–89 Lots Road
London SW10 0RN
Tel: 020 7349 9999
Fax: 020 7349 0410
interiors@todhunterearle.com
www.todhunterearle.com
Page 52br.

TOUCH INTERIOR DESIGN
Tel: 020 7498 6409
Pages 72ac, 72ar, 96bl.

JIM TRIBE
General Contractor for Orman project
Temple Contracting
20 West 20th Street
New York NY 10011
USA
Pages 8b, 20ac, 89bl, 98ar, 124r, 135r, 140br, 143a, 148r, 171ar, 173l.

TSAO & MCKOWN
Architects
20 Vandam Street, 10th Floor
New York NY 10013
Tel: +1 212 337 3800
Fax: +1 212 337 0013
Pages 159l, 163b, 165cl, 168bl.

TSÉ TSÉ AT GALERIE SENTOU
26 boulevard Raspail
75007 Paris
France
Tel: +33 1 45 49 00 05
and at
Maryse Boxer Design
26 Sloane Street
London SW1X 7QL
Tel: 020 7 245 9493
Elegant, quirky lighting designs by a stylish young French company
Pages 49l, 130al.

URBAN RESEARCH LABORATORY
3 Plantain Place
Crosby Row
London SE1 1YN
Tel: 020 7403 2929
jeff@urbanresearchlab.com
Pages 10, 16br, 127r, 134, 135bl, 139cl, 142br, 159br.

URBAN SALON
Architects
Unit D
Flat Iron Yard
Ayres Street
London SE1 1ES
Tel: 020 7357 8000
Page 108bc.

VX DESIGN & ARCHITECTURE
www.vxdesign.com
vx@vxdesign.com
Tel/fax: 020 7370 5496
Pages 2ac, 2c, 4a, 18b, 28b, 32, 34l, 36br, 45ar, 55al, 75ar, 84, 85al, 129ac, 144al, 144ar, 157ar, 163a, 172cr, 173r.

STEPHEN VARADY ARCHITECTURE
Studio 5
102 Albion StreetSurry Hills
2010 Sydney
New South Wales
Australia
Tel: +61 2 9281 4825
Page 41b.

HÉRVE VERMESCH
50 rue Bichat
75010 Paris
France
Tel: +33 1 42 01 39 39
Pages 85ar, 146cl.

OLIVIER VIDAL AND ASSOCIATES
(ARCHITECTS)
14 rue Moncey
75009 Paris
France
Pages 68a, 80bl.

BERNARD M. WHARTON
Shope Reno Wharton Associates
18 West Putnam Avenue
Greenwich CT 06830
Tel: +1 203 869 7250
srwol@aol.com
www.shoperenowharton.com
Page 94br.

HEIDI WISH AND PHILIP WISH
Interior Design & Build
Tel/fax: 0207 737 7797
Pages 159ar, 162ar, 166ar.

VICENTE WOLF ASSOCIATES, INC.
333 West 39th Street
New York NY 10018
USA
Tel: +1 212 465 0590
Page 94bl.

VOON WONG ARCHITECTS
Unit 27
1 Stannary Street
London SW11 4AD
Tel: 020 7587 0116
Fax: 020 7840 0178
voon@dircon.co.uk
Pages 33al, 48, 138.

STEPHEN WOODHAM
Woodhams Ltd
Tel: 020 8964 9818
Pages 153bl, 154ar.

WOOLF ARCHITECTS
39–51 Highgate Road
London NW5 1RT
Tel: 020 7428 9500
Pages 43b, 82b, 113cl, 115c.

YVES-CLAUDE DESIGN
Architectural/industrial design firm specializing in stainless-steel kitchens, furniture and interiors
199 Layfayette Street
New York NY 10012
USA
info@kanso.com
www.kanso.com
Pages 3l, 142c, 144br, 145cl, 145br, 149a, 153al, 153ac.

CONSUELO ZOELLY
5–7 rue Mont Louis
75011 Paris
France
Tel: +33 42 62 19 95
Page 142bl.

picture credits

All photographs by Chris Everard unless otherwise stated.
Key: ph=photographer, a=above, b=below, r=right, l=left, c=centre.

1 Interior Designer Angela Kearsey's house in London-architectural design by Dols Wong Architects, interior design by Angela Kearsey; **2al** Hudson Street Loft designed by Moneo Brock Studio; **2ac** Ian Chee of VX design & architecture; **2ar&cl** Michael Nathenson's house in London; **2c** Ian Chee of VX design & architecture; **2cr** Interior Designer Angela Kearsey's house in London-architectural design by Dols Wong Architects, interior design by Angela Kearsey; **2bl** ph Alan Williams/Private apartment in London designed by Hugh Broughton Architects; **2br** ph Henry Bourne/Richard Mabb and Kate Green's apartment in London; **3l** Vicson Guevara's apartment in New York designed by Yves-Claude; **3c&r** Charles Bateson's house in London; **4a** Ian Chee of VX design & architecture; **4b** Nadav Kander & Nicole Verity's house; **5** A loft in London designed by Eger Architects; **6al** Hudson Street Loft designed by Moneo Brock Studio; **6ac** Charles Bateson's house in London; **6ar** ph Henry Bourne; **6cl** Ruth Artmonsky's loft in Covent Garden; **6bl** ph James Merrell; **6br** Interior Designer Angela Kearsey's house in London-architectural design by Dols Wong Architects, interior design by Angela Kearsey; **7a** Photographer Guy Hills' studio in London designed by Retrouvius; **7c** Designed by Filer & Cox, London; **7b** ph James Merrell/a house in Sydney designed by Interni Interior Design Consultancy; **8a** John Barman's Park Avenue Apartment; **8c** designed by Mullman Seidman Architects; **8b** Suze Orman's apartment in New York designed by Patricia Seidman of Mullman Seidman Architects; **9al** Nadav Kander & Nicole Verity's house; **9ar** a loft in London designed by Eger Architects; **9bl** ph Andrew Wood/A house in London designed by Bowles and Linares; **9bc** Freddie Daniells' apartment in London designed by Brookes Stacey Randall; **9cr** a house in Hampstead, London designed by Orefelt Associates; **9br** Charles Bateson's house in London; **10** ph Alan Williams/Richard Oyarzarbal's apartment in London designed by Urban Research Laboratory; **11al** A loft in London designed by Eger Architects; **11bl** ph James Morris/'The Peg Yorkin House' by Moore Ruble Yudell Architects & Planners. Principal in charge Buzz Yudell, Principal Designer John Ruble, Project Architect Marc Schoeplein; **11r** ph Tom Leighton/Sally Butler's house in London; **12** ph James Merrell/designed by Interni Interior Design Consultancy; **12–13** ph Henry Bourne/a house in London designed by Charles Rutherfoord; **13** ph Ray Main/Jonathan Leitersdorf's apartment in New York designed by Jonathan Leitersdorf/Just Design Ltd; **14al** ph Catherine Gratwicke/Johanne Riss' house in Brussels; **14ar** ph Andrew Wood/Pete & Connie di Girolamo house in San Diego; **14bl** The loft of Mary and Sean Kelly designed by Steven Learner Studio; **14bc** Dominique Lubar for IPL Interiors; **14br** Andrew Wood/Philip and Barbara Silver's house in Idaho designed by Mark Pynn A.I.A. of McMillen Pynn Architecture L.L.P.; **15l** ph Andrew Wood/Isosceles Land Pte Ltd's house in Singapore designed by Chan Soo Khian of SCDA Architects; **15c** ph Ray Main/Gisela Garson's house in Stoke Newington designed by FAT; **15r** ph Alan Williams/The Arbuthnott family's house near Cirencester designed by Nicholas Arbuthnott, fabrics designed by Vanessa Arbuthnott; **16a** Nadav Kander & Nicole Verity's house; **16bl** ph James Merrell/a house in Queensland designed by Tony Suttle; **16bc** ph Tom Leighton/Sally Butler's house in London; **16br** ph Alan Williams/Richard Oyarzarbal's apartment in London designed by Urban Research Laboratory; **17** ph Christopher Drake/Juan Corbella's apartment in London designed by HM2, Richard Webb with Andrew Hanson; **18al&r** Hudson Street Loft designed by Moneo Brock Studio; **18b** Ian Chee of VX design & architecture; **19al** John Barman's Park Avenue Apartment; **19ac&ar** Garden Room, London for David & Anne Harriss designed by Eger Architects; **19cl** Michael Nathenson's house in London; **19bl** Charles Bateson's house in London; **19br** Interior Designer Angela Kearsey's house in London-architectural design by Dols Wong Architects, interior design by Angela Kearsey; **20al** Michael Nathenson's house in London; **20ac** Suze Orman's apartment in New York designed by Patricia Seidman of Mullman Seidman Architects; **20ar** ph Andrew Wood/A house in London designed by Bowles and Linares; **20cl** Designed by Filer & Cox, London; **20c** A loft in London

designed by Eger Architects; **20cr** Michael Nathenson's house in London; **20bl** ph James Merrell/Sophie Sarin's flat in London; **20bc** ph James Merrell/Paula Pryke and Peter Romaniuk's house in London; **20br** ph David Montgomery/The Montevetro apartment in London designed by David Collins, photographed courtesy of Taylor Woodrow Capital Developments Ltd; **21a** ph James Merrell/Grant Ford and Jane Bailey's house in London/kitchen by Rhode Design; **21c** Charles Bateson's house in London; **21b** ph James Merrell/Sally Butler's house in London; **22** Photographer Guy Hills' studio in London designed by Retrouvius; **22–23** Nadav Kander & Nicole Verity's house; **23** The London apartment of the Sheppard Day Design Partnership; **24al** A loft in London designed by Eger Architects; **24ac** ph Alan Williams/Stanley & Nancy Grossman's apartment in New York designed by Jennifer Post Design; **24ar** ph James Morris/an atelier in Paris designed by Damien Roland; **24c** ph James Morris/'The Peg Yorkin House' by Moore Ruble Yudell Architects & Planners. Principal in charge Buzz Yudell, Principal Designer John Ruble, Project Architect Marc Schoeplein; **24b** ph James Morris/House in Harrison, New York, designed by Sidnam Petrone Gartner Architects; **25a** ph James Morris/A House in Wiltshire designed by Ken Shuttleworth; **25c** James Morris/A Mountain House in Georgia designed by Mack Scogin Merrill Elam Architects; **25b** ph Ray Main/Robert Callender & Elizabeth Ogilvie's studio in Fife designed by John C Hope Architects; **26a** ph James Morris/The Jackee' and Elgin Charles House in California's Hollywood Hills, designed by William R. Heffner AIA, interior design by Sandy Davidson Design; **26–27a** James Morris/The Lew House, originally designed by Richard Neutra in 1958, architect and contractor Marmol Radziner + Associates, Architecture and Construction; **26–27b** James Morris/Skywood House near London designed by Graham Phillips; **27** ph James Morris/Upper East Side Townhouse in New York City designed by Ogawa/Depardon Architects; **28al&ac** a loft in London designed by Eger Architects; **28ar** Photographer Guy Hills' studio in London designed by Retrouvius; **28b** Ian Chee of VX design & architecture; **29al** ph Ray Main/Jamie Falla's house in London designed by MOOArc; **29ar** ph James Morris/House refurbishment in North London, Mark Guard Architects; **29br** Charles Bateson's house in London; **30al** ph Ray Main/Jonathan Reed's apartment in London; **30c** Ray Main/an apartment in London designed by Brookes Stacey Randall; **30ar** Garden Room, London for David & Anne Harriss designed by Eger Architects; **30bl** ph Andrew Wood/Namly Drive house in Singapore designed by Juan Peck Foon; **30br** Ruth Artmonsky's loft in Covent Garden; **31** ph Ray Main/an apartment in London designed by Brookes Stacey Randall; **32** Ian Chee of VX design & architecture; **33al** ph Alan Williams/The architect Voon Wong's own apartment in London; **33bl** ph Henry Bourne/Frédéric Méchiche's apartment in Paris; **33r** ph Catherine Gratwicke/Agnès Emery's house in Brussels, tiles from Emery & Cie; **34l** Ian Chee of VX design & architecture; **34c** ph Henry Bourne/a house in Devon designed by Anthony Hudson of Hudson Featherstone Architects; **34–35** ph Ray Main/Client's residence, East Hampton, New York, designed by ZG DESIGN; **35al** ph James Merrell/an apartment in New York designed by Campion A Platt Architect; **35ar** ph Henry Bourne/Linda Trahair's house in Bath; **35c&bl** Photographer Guy Hills' studio in London designed by Retrouvius; **35br** ph Ray Main/Thierry Watorek's house near Paris; **36al** ph Henry Bourne/Felix Bonnier's apartment in New York; **36ar** Charles Bateson's house in London; **36bl** ph James Merrell/a house in Sydney designed by Luigi Rosselli; **36br** Ian Chee of VX design & architecture; **37a** ph Henry Bourne/a mews house in London designed by McDowell & Benedetti; **37b** ph Henry Bourne; **38al&br** ph Henry Bourne; **38ar** ph James Merrell; **38bl** ph James Merrell/a house in London designed by François Gilles & Dominique Lubar, IPL Interiors; **38–39 & 39bl** James Merrell/a terrace in London designed by Christophe Gollut; **39ar** ph Catherine Gratwicke/Agnès Emery's house in Brussels, tiles from Emery & Cie; **39br** ph James Merrell/a house in Sydney designed by Interni Interior Design Consultancy; **40** ph James Morris/an atelier in Paris designed by Damien Roland; **41a** ph Henry Bourne/a mews house in London designed by Architect McDowell & Benedetti; **41c** ph Henry Bourne/Charles Rutherfoord's house in London; **41b** ph James Merrell/Amanda and Andrew Manning's apartment in Sydney designed by Stephen Varady Architecture; **42al** ph Ray Main/Robert Callender & Elizabeth Ogilvie's studio in Fife designed by John C Hope Architects; **42ar** ph Henry Bourne/a loft in London designed by Robert Dye Associates; **42b** ph Henry Bourne/DAD Associates; **43a** ph Henry Bourne/a house in

London designed by Mark Guard Architects; **43b** ph Henry Bourne/a house in London designed by Woolf architects; **44** Designed by Filer & Cox, London; **45al** a loft in London designed by Eger Architects; **45ac** ph Henry Bourne/Frédéric Méchiche's apartment in Paris; **45ar** Ian Chee of VX design & architecture; **45b** Henry Bourne/a house in Devon designed by Anthony Hudson of Hudson Featherstone Architects; **46a** all Henry Bourne/a house in London designed by Charles Rutherfoord; **46bl** Ray Main/Thierry Watorek's house near Paris; **46br** ph James Merrell; **47** Nadav Kander & Nicole Verity's house; **48** ph Alan Williams/The architect Voon Wong's own apartment in London; **49l** ph Ray Main/lights by Tsé Tsé associées, Catherine Levy and Sigolène Prébois; **49c** ph Ray Main/Evan Snyderman's house in Brooklyn; **49r** ph Alan Williams/Jennifer & Geoffrey Symonds' apartment in New York designed by Jennifer Post Design; **50al** Andrew Wilson's apartment in London designed by Azman Owens; **50ar** ph Alan Williams/Private apartment in London designed by Hugh Broughton Architects; **50b** ph James Merrell/Victor Ktori's loft in London designed by Circus Architects; **51** Designer Karim Rashid's own apartment in New York; **52al** ph Henry Bourne/John Raab's apartment in London/floor by Sinclair Till; **52ar** ph Henry Bourne/a house in London designed by Charles Rutherfoord; **52bl** ph James Merrell/Sue and Andy's apartment in Blackheath; **52br** ph Henry Bourne/an apartment in London designed by Emily Todhunter; **53al** ph Henry Bourne/Dan and Claire Thorne's town house in Dorset designed by Sarah Featherstone of Hudson Featherstone Architects; **53ar** ph Henry Bourne/floor by Dalsouple, First Floor; **53bl** ph Henry Bourne/Circus Architects/floor by First Floor; **53br** ph Henry Bourne/Richard Mabb and Kate Green's apartment in London; **54al** ph Henry Bourne/Roger and Fay Oates' house in Eastnor; **54ac** ph James Merrell/rug designed by Christine Vanderhurd; **54ar** ph James Merrell; **54cr** ph Andrew Wood/Roger and Fay Oates' house in Eastnor; **54–55b** ph Henry Bourne/floor by Helen Yardley; **55al** Ian Chee of VX design & architecture; **55ar** Charles Bateson's house in London; **55cr** ph James Merrell; **55br** ph Henry Bourne/an apartment in London designed by Ash Sakula Architects/rug by Christopher Farr; **56** ph Andrew Wood/Roger and Suzy Black's apartment in London designed by Johnson Naylor; **57l** ph Ray Main/a loft in London designed by Circus Architects; **57c** ph Andrew Wood/Phil and Gail Handy's house in Idaho designed by Mark Pynn A.I.A. of McMillen Pynn Architecture L.L.P.; **57r** ph James Morris/a house near Brussels designed by Claire Bataille & Paul ibens; **58** ph Andrew Wood/Alastair Hendy & John Clinch's apartment in London designed by Alastair Hendy; **58–59** ph Andrew Wood/Nik Randall, Suzsi Corio and Louis' home in London designed by Brookes Stacey Randall; **59** Photographer Guy Hills' studio in London designed by Retrouvius; **60al&cl** ph Ray Main/a loft in London designed by Circus Architects; **60bl** ph Ray Main/Seth Stein's house in London; **60r** ph James Morris/a house near Brussels designed by Claire Bataille & Paul ibens; **61ar** ph Ray Main/an apartment in London designed by Circus Architects; **61c** An apartment in New York designed by Gabellini Associates; **61bl&br** John Eldridge's loft apartment in London designed by Seth Stein; **62l** ph Andrew Wood; **62r** ph Ray Main/David Mellor's home and studio at Hathersage in Derbyshire; **62–63** ph Ray Main/Kenneth Hirst's apartment in New York; **64al** ph Andrew Wood/Phil and Gail Handy's house in Idaho designed by Mark Pynn A.I.A. of McMillen Pynn Architecture L.L.P.; **64ar** ph James Morris/Nomentana Residence in Maine designed by Mack Scogin Merrill Elam Architects; **64bl** ph Andrew Wood/an apartment in Bath designed by Briffa Phillips Architects; **64bc** ph Andrew Wood/Media executive's house in Los Angeles, Architect: Stephen Slan, Builder: Ken Duran, Furnishings: Russell Simpson, Original Architect: Carl Maston c.1945; **64br** ph Ray Main/John Howell's loft in London designed by Circus Architects; **65** ph Ray Main/a loft in London designed by Circus Architects; **66a&cr** ph Andrew Wood/An apartment in London designed by James Gorst; **66cl** ph Andrew Wood/Roger and Suzy Black's apartment in London designed by Johnson Naylor; **66b** ph Tom Leighton/armoire & chair Josephine Ryan; **67al** ph Ray Main/Mr & Mrs Cordier's home, Church Farm Oast, near Horsmonden, Kent, UK; **67ar** ph Andrew Wood/Richard and Sue Hare's house in Idaho designed by Mark Pynn A.I.A. of McMillen Pynn Architecture L.L.P.; **67bl** ph Chris Tubbs/Nickerson-Wakefield House in upstate New York/anderson architects; **67br** ph Ray Main/Marina & Peter Hill's barn in West Sussex designed by Marina Hill, Peter James Construction Management, Chichester, The West Sussex Antique Timber Company, Wisborough Green, and Joanna Jefferson Architects;

68a&b ph James Merrell; **68–69** ph Andrew Wood/Media executive's house in Los Angeles, Architect: Stephen Slan, Builder: Ken Duran, Furnishings: Russell Simpson, Original Architect: Carl Maston c. 1945; **70a** ph Alan Williams/Andrew Wallace's house in London; **70c** ph Tom Leighton; **70b** ph Alan Williams/Interior Designer Roberto Bergero's own apartment in Paris; **71a** all Dominique Lubar for IPL Interiors; **71cl** François Muracciole's apartment in Paris; **71bl** ph Andrew Wood/an apartment in The San Remo on the Upper West Side of Manhattan, designed by John L. Stewart and Michael D'Arcy of SIT; **71br** Nadav Kander & Nicole Verity's house; **72al&bl** Designed by Filer & Cox, London; **72ac&ar** ph Alan Williams/Katie Bassford King's house in London designed by Touch Interior Design; **73al** ph Ray Main/a house in Pennsylvania designed by Jeffrey Bilhuber; **73bl** Designed by Filer & Cox, London; **73a&br & 74** Nadav Kander & Nicole Verity's house; **75l** ph James Morris/a house in London designed by Alan Power; **75ar** Ian Chee of VX design & architecture; **75br** Ray Main/Lee F. Mindel's apartment in New York, designed by Shelton, Mindel & Associates with Associate Architect Reed Morrison, lighting design by Johnson Schwinghammer; **76a** ph James Morris/Upper East Side Townhouse in New York City designed by Ogawa/Depardon Architects; **76b** ph James Morris/a house in London designed by Alan Power; **77** ph Ray Main/Lee F. Mindel's apartment in New York, designed by Shelton, Mindel & Associates with Associate Architect Reed Morrison, lighting design by Johnson Schwinghammer; **78l** ph Ray Main/an apartment in London designed by Circus Architects; **78r** ph James Morris/The Jackee' and Elgin Charles House in California's Hollywood Hills, designed by William R. Heffner AIA, interior design by Sandy Davidson Design; **79 both** ph James Morris/Upper East Side Townhouse in New York City designed by Ogawa/Depardon Architects; **80bl** ph James Merrell; **80bc** Ruth Artmonsky's loft in Covent Garden; **80a&br** Nadav Kander & Nicole Verity's house; **81l** ph James Morris/The Lew House, originally designed by Richard Neutra in 1958, architect and contractor Marmol Radziner + Associates, Architecture and Construction **81r** Photographer Guy Hills' studio in London designed by Retrouvius; **82a** ph Henry Bourne/a house in Devon designed by Anthony Hudson of Hudson Featherstone Architects; **82b** ph Henry Bourne/a house in London designed by Woolf architects; **83** ph James Morris/a house in London designed by Alan Power; **84 & 85al** Ian Chee of VX design & architecture; **85ac** ph Ray Main/Lee F. Mindel's apartment in New York, designed by Shelton, Mindel & Associates with Associate Architect Reed Morrison, lighting design by Johnson Schwinghammer; **85ar** ph Ray Main/a house in Paris designed by Hervé Vermesch; **85c** ph Ray Main/Kirk & Caroline Pickering's house in London, space creation by Square Foot Properties Ltd; **85cr** ph Ray Main/Mr & Mrs Cordier's home, Church Farm Oast, near Horsmonden, Kent, UK; **85br** ph Ray Main/Robert Callender & Elizabeth Ogilvie's studio in Fife designed by John C Hope Architects; **86l** ph Andrew Wood/Jamie Falla's house in London designed by MOOArc; **86ar&br** ph Andrew Wood/a house near Antwerp designed by Claire Bataille and Paul ibens; **87** ph Henry Bourne/a house in Devon designed by Anthony Hudson of Hudson Featherstone Architects; **88** Hudson Street Loft designed by Moneo Brock Studio; **89al** Dominique Lubar for IPL Interiors; **89bl** Suze Orman's apartment in New York designed by Patricia Seidman of Mullman Seidman Architects; **89c&r** Michael Nathenson's house in London; **90** Charles Bateson's house in London; **91al** Interior Designer Angela Kearsey's house in London-architectural design by Dols Wong Architects, interior design by Angela Kearsey; **91ar** ph Andrew Wood/An apartment in London designed by James Gorst; **91bl** The London apartment of the Sheppard Day Design Partnership; **91bc** ph Andrew Wood/Jamie Falla's house in London designed by MOOArc; **91br** Dominique Lubar for IPL Interiors; **92 & 93al** Michael Nathenson's house in London; **93ar** Hudson Street Loft designed by Moneo Brock Studio; **93br** Nadav Kander & Nicole Verity's house; **94a** ph Polly Wreford/Sheila Scholes & Gunter Schmidt's house in Cambridgeshire; **94bl** ph Ray Main/a house in East Hampton, interior by Vicente Wolf; **94br** ph Chris Tubbs/A cottage in Connecticut designed by Benard M. Wharton; **95** Dominique Lubar for IPL Interiors; **96al** ph Andrew Wood/The Glendale, California, home of John & Heather Banfield; **96bl** ph Alan Williams/Katie Bassford King's house in London designed by Touch Interior Design; **96—97** ph Alan Williams/Owner of Gloss, Pascale Bredillet's own apartment in London; **97** ph Alan Williams/Warner Johnson's apartment in New York designed by Edward Cabot of Cabot Design Ltd.; **98al** ph Andrew Wood/Evelyne Roussel's house in Paris; **98ac**

142a ph Alan Williams/Maria Jesus Polanco's apartment in New York designed by Hut Sachs Studio in collaboration with Moneo Brock Studio; **142cl** ph James Merrell/kitchen by Rhode Design; **142c** Vicson Guevara's apartment in New York designed by Yves-Claude; **142cr** Designed by Filer & Cox, London; **142bl** ph James Merrell/Consuelo Zoelly's apartment in Paris; **142bc** Charles Bateson's house in London; **142br** ph Alan Williams/Richard Oyarzarbal's apartment in London designed by Urban Research Laboratory; **143a** Suze Orman's apartment in New York designed by Patricia Seidman of Mullman Seidman Architects; **143b** designed by Mullman Seidman Architects; **144al&ar** Ian Chee of VX design & architecture; **144br** Vicson Guevara's apartment in New York designed by Yves-Claude; **145al** ph Alan Williams/Private apartment in London designed by Hugh Broughton Architects; **145ar** Designer Karim Rashid's own apartment in New York; **145bl** John Barman's Park Avenue Apartment; **145cl&br** Vicson Guevara's apartment in New York designed by Yves-Claude; **146al** ph James Merrell/a house in London designed by Ash Sakula Architects; **146ac** ph Christopher Drake/Melanie Thornton's house in Gloucestershire; **146ar** ph James Merrell; **146cl** ph James Merrell/an apartment in Paris designed by Hervé Vermesch; **146c** ph Ray Main/Marie-Pierre Morel's house in Paris designed by François Muracciole; **146cr** Sig.ra Venturini's apartment in Milan; **146bl** ph James Merrell/Felix Bonnier's apartment in Paris; **146bc** ph James Merrell/Sophie Sarin's flat in London; **146br** ph Andrew Wood/Curtice Booth's house in Pasadena, California; **147a** Hudson Street Loft designed by Moneo Brock Studio; **147c** ph Christopher Drake/Refurbishment and interior design by Chicchi Meroni Fassio, Parnassus; **147b** ph James Merrell/Sussie Ahlburg and Andy Keate's house in London; **148al** ph Polly Wreford/Lena Proudlock's house in Gloucestershire; **148bl** François Muracciole's apartment in Paris; **148r** Suze Orman's apartment in New York designed by Patricia Seidman of Mullman Seidman Architects; **149l** Michael Nathenson's house in London; **149a** Vicson Guevara's apartment in New York designed by Yves-Claude; **149br** Kampfner's house in London designed by Ash Sakula Architects; **150a,bl&bc** John Barman's Park Avenue Apartment; **150br** ph Andrew Wood; **151al&ac** Hudson Street Loft designed by Moneo Brock Studio **151ar** Arlene Hirst's New York Kitchen designed by Steven Sclaroff; **151b** Designer Karim Rashid's own apartment in New York; **152a** John Barman's Park Avenue Apartment; **152bl** ph James Merrell/Mike and Kris Taylor's loft in London designed by Circus Architects with Kayode Lipede; **152br** designed by Mullman Seidman Architects; **153al&ac** Vicson Guevara's apartment in New York designed by Yves-Claude; **153ar** Michael Nathenson's house in London; **153cl** Hudson Street Loft designed by Moneo Brock Studio; **153bl** ph James Merrell/Stephen Woodham's house in London designed in conjunction with Mark Brook Design; **153br** designed by Mullman Seidman Architects; **154al** ph Alan Williams/The Arbuthnott family's house near Cirencester designed by Nicholas Arbuthnott, fabrics designed by Vanessa Arbuthnott; **154ac** ph James Merrell/Ash Sakula's house in London; **154ar** ph James Merrell/Stephen Woodham's house in London designed in conjunction with Mark Brook Design; **154bl** Designed by Filer & Cox, London; **154—155b & 155c** Hudson Street Loft designed by Moneo Brock Studio; **155al** Arlene Hirst's New York Kitchen designed by Steven Sclaroff; **155ac** a house in London designed by Ash Sakula Architects; **155ar** ph James Merrell/Linda Parham and David Slobham's apartment in Sydney designed by architect Stephen Varady; **155b** ph James Merrell/Rose Gray's flat in London designed by Hester Gray; **156** a house in Hampstead, London designed by Orefelt Associates; **157al** John Barman's Park Avenue Apartment; **157ac** Designed by Filer & Cox, London; **157ar** Ian Chee of VX design & architecture; **157b** designed by Mullman Seidman Architects; **158al** ph James Morris/A house in London designed by Azman Owens Architects; **158ar** Philippa Rose's house in London designed by Caroline Paterson/Victoria Fairfax of Paterson Gornall Interiors, together with Clive Butcher Designs; **158cl** ph Henry Bourne/a house in London designed by Charles Rutherfoord; **158bl** ph Andrew Wood/An apartment in London designed by James Gorst; **158br** Charles Bateson's house in London; **159l** Calvin Tsao & Zack McKown's apartment in New York designed by Tsao & McKown; **159ar** Heidi Wish & Philip Wish's apartment in London designed by Moutarde & Heidi Wish; **159br** ph Alan Williams/Richard Oyarzarbal's apartment in London designed by Urban Research Laboratory; **160a** ph Alan Williams/Hudson Street Loft in New York designed by Moneo Brock Studio; **160cl** Karen Davies' apartment in London designed by Joëlle Darby;

160bl John Eldridge's loft apartment in London designed by Seth Stein; **160bc** an apartment in Paris designed by Bruno Tanquerel; **160br** One New Inn Square, a private dining room and home of chef David Vanderhook, all enquiries (020 7729 3645); **161a** ph James Morris/'The Jackee' and Elgin Charles House in California's Hollywood Hills, designed by William R. Heffner AIA, interior design by Sandy Davidson Design; **161bl** ph James Morris/A loft apartment in London designed by Simon Conder Associates; **161bc** The London apartment of the Sheppard Day Design Partnership; **161br** a house in Hampstead, London designed by Orefelt Associates; **162al** Michael Nathenson's house in London; **162ac** Freddie Daniells' apartment in London designed by Brookes Stacey Randall; **162ar** Heidi Wish & Philip Wish's apartment in London designed by Moutarde & Heidi Wish; **162bl** a house in Hampstead, London designed by Orefelt Associates; **162cr** House in London by Seth Stein; **162br** Designed by Filer & Cox, London; **163a** Ian Chee of VX design & architecture; **163b** Calvin Tsao & Zack McKown's apartment in New York designed by Tsao & McKown; **164l** Emma & Neil's house in London, walls painted by Garth Carter; **164r** A loft apartment in London designed by Simon Conder Associates; **165al** Suzanne Slesin & Michael Steinberg's apartment in New York – design by Jean-Louis Ménard; **165cl** Calvin Tsao & Zack McKown's apartment in New York designed by Tsao & McKown; **165bl** a house in Highbury, London designed by Dale Loth Architects; **165ar** John Barman's Park Avenue Apartment; **165bc** architect's house in London designed by Dale Loth Architects; **165br** Simon Brignall & Christina Rosetti's loft apartment in London designed by David Mikhail Architects; **166al** New York City apartment designed by Marino + Giolito; **166ac** Charles Bateson's house in London; **166ar** Heidi Wish & Philip Wish's apartment in London designed by Moutarde & Heidi Wish; **166cl** Richard Hopkin's apartment in London designed by HM2; **166c** an apartment in New York designed by David Deutsch & Sidnam Petrone Gartner Architects; **166cr** Architect Nigel Smith's apartment in London; **166bl** One New Inn Square, a private dining room and home of chef David Vanderhook, all enquiries (020 7729 3645); **166bc&br** a house in Paris designed by Bruno Tanquerel; **167a** Hudson Street Loft designed by Moneo Brock Studio; **167c** Nadav Kander & Nicole Verity's house; **167b & 168al** John Eldridge's loft apartment in London designed by Seth Stein; **168ar** Charles Bateson's house in London; **168bl** Calvin Tsao & Zack McKown's apartment in New York designed by Tsao & McKown; **168br** Paul Brazier & Diane Lever's house in London designed by Carden & Cunietti; **169al** a house in Paris designed by Bruno Tanquerel; **169ac** ph Andrew Wood/Alastair Hendy & John Clinch's apartment in London designed by Alastair Hendy; **169ar** Sera Hersham-Loftus' house in London; **169cr** architect's house in London designed by Dale Loth Architects; **169br** a house in London designed by Carden & Cunietti; **170al** Simon Brignall & Christina Rosetti's loft apartment in London designed by David Mikhail Architects; **170ar** a house in Hampstead, London designed by Orefelt Associates; **170c** New York City apartment designed by Marino + Giolito; **170b** Designed by Filer & Cox, London; **171al** Jacques & Laurence Hintzy's apartment near Paris designed by Paul Mathieu; **171ac** Michael Nathenson's house in London; **171ar** Suze Orman's apartment in New York designed by Patricia Seidman of Mullman Seidman Architects; **171b** designed by Mullman Seidman Architects; **172al** ph Andrew Wood/A house at Jalan Berjaya, Singapore designed by Chan Soo Khian of SCDA Architects; **172ac** ph Andrew Wood/Roger and Suzy Black's apartment in London designed by Johnson Naylor; **172ar** Michael Nathenson's house in London; **172cl** Gentucca Bini's apartment in Milan; **172c** ph Henry Bourne/a loft in London designed by DAD Associates; **172cr** Ian Chee of VX design & architecture; **172bl** Designed by Filer & Cox, London; **172bc** ph Andrew Wood/A house near Antwerp designed by Claire Bataille and Paul ibens; **172br** ph Andrew Wood/Media executive's house in Los Angeles, Architect: Stephen Slan, Builder: Ken Duran, Furnishings: Russell Simpson, Original Architect: Carl Maston c. 1945; **173l** Suze Orman's apartment in New York designed by Patricia Seidman of Mullman Seidman Architects; **173c** ph Alan Williams/Alannah Weston's house in London designed by Stickland Coombe Architecture; **173r** Ian Chee of VX design & architecture.

In addition to the designers and owners mentioned above we would also like to thank Katsuji Asada and garden antiques expert Peter Hone.

index

Figures in *italics* indicate captions.

acknowledgments

Compiling this book has reinforced my admiration for architects and designers, their breadth of knowledge, imagination and sheer resourcefulness. It is not entirely reasonable to ask professionals to give up hard-won information, but I would like to thank all of those who so generously shared their trade secrets. Thanks, too, must go to my friend and colleague Caroline Rodrigues for her help and encouragement, to Sophie Bevan for her patience, calm and good-humour and to Sally Powell and the rest of the creative team at Ryland Peters & Small for making this book look so wonderful.